This was the most helpful book I have read all year! *Inspired by the Psalms* uniquely combines Elizabeth A. Nixon's legal expertise with her deep insight into life-changing biblical principles. It will change your life! I saw changes happen almost immediately!

—DOUG ADDISON
WWW.DOUGADDISON.COM, INLIGHT CONNECTION
LOS ANGELES, CALIFORNIA

In a world that continues to face seemingly insurmountable challenges, the need for powerful, creative, life-changing, spoken words is desperate. *Inspired by the Psalms* by Elizabeth A. Nixon provides just that. Words hold the power to change atmospheres and create opportunities of hope and destiny. Elizabeth has captured the moment in this book.

Inspired by the Psalms will not only lift the human spirit but also define purpose, future, and strategies for the reader. Prophetic declarations to take mountains of influence will cause positive, advancing change in the world we live in. I love this book, and I strongly recommend *Inspired by the Psalms* for everyone who is determined to triumph in life.

—CINDY MCGILL
AUTHOR, SPEAKER, PROPHETIC DREAM INTERPRETER

There's something powerful that happens when the Word of God is released as a spiritual decree. There's a majestic anointing; there's a shift into a regal anointing that shatters and penetrates the second heavens and brings transformation to the earth. When our spirits, souls, and bodies are in divine order and we decree the power of God's Word, using the examples in this wonderful book, be expectant and be ready—transformation occurs!

Meditate on the truths in this book so that when you decree the Psalms, they come forth from your spirit and literally bring the kingdom of God to earth. Elizabeth A. Nixon has brought forth a timely truth and teaching for the seasons that are facing the church in the time to come.

—SUZETTE TORTI
AGENT OF CHANGE/PASTOR,
OPEN HEAVEN MINISTRIES INTERNATIONAL LTD.
WWW.OPENHEAVEN.ORG.AU
GOLD COAST, AUSTRALIA

In this timely book Elizabeth A. Nixon provides a series of scripturally based decrees you can use to build your future. Speak wisely, love ardently, and watch God intervene gloriously in your life.

—JOAN HUNTER
JOAN HUNTER MINISTRIES
WWW.JOANHUNTER.ORG
PINEHURST, TEXAS

Scripture says that we have the power of life and death in our tongue (Prov. 18:21). We can actually use our tongue to release life over ourselves, our families, our homes, our work, our communities, our spheres of influence, and the list could go on. If only the church would grab hold of this and live it out daily!

Keys to this kind of living are found in *Inspired by the Psalms*. Read it; meditate on it; most importantly, speak these life-giving decrees out over your life. The atmosphere around you will change. God's Word will not return void. And you will witness the power of life being released in you and around you in awe-inspiring ways!

—JEANNINE RODRIGUEZ-EVERARD
IMAGES OF LIGHT
WWW.IMAGESOFLIGHT.US

When confronted with adverse situations in His life, or someone else's, Jesus consistently reached into the truths of Psalms and applied those truths with amazing results. He declared them throughout His life and ministry. Their priceless and poetic promises not only kept Him in life, but they also provided Him the appropriate revelation at His death. For at the darkest moment in human history He spoke a psalm. Thank you, Elizabeth A. Nixon, for this profound and revelatory reminder of the value of eternal truths applied to every situation that we face.

—RAY HUGHES
SELAH MINISTRIES
WWW.SELAHMINISTRIES.COM
ASHEVILLE, NORTH CAROLINA

INSPIRED
by the
Psalms

ELIZABETH A. NIXON, ESQ

CHARISMA
HOUSE

Most CHARISMA HOUSE BOOK GROUP products are available at special quantity discounts for bulk purchase for sales promotions, premiums, fund-raising, and educational needs. For details, write Charisma House Book Group, 600 Rinehart Road, Lake Mary, Florida 32746, or telephone (407) 333-0600.

INSPIRED BY THE PSALMS by Elizabeth A. Nixon, Esq.
Published by Charisma House
Charisma Media/Charisma House Book Group
600 Rinehart Road
Lake Mary, Florida 32746
www.charismahouse.com

Unless otherwise noted, all Scripture quotations are from the King James Version of the Bible.

Scripture quotations marked AMP are from the Amplified Bible. Old Testament copyright © 1965, 1987 by the Zondervan Corporation. The Amplified New Testament copyright © 1954, 1958, 1987 by the Lockman Foundation. Used by permission.

Scripture quotations marked DARBY are from the Darby Translation of the Holy Bible. Public domain.

Scripture quotations marked KJ21 are taken from the 21st Century King James Version, copyright © 1994. Used by permission of Deuel Enterprises, Inc., Gary, SD 57237. All rights reserved.

Scripture quotations marked NAS are from the New American Standard Bible, copyright © 1960, 1962, 1963, 1968, 1971, 1972, 1973, 1975, 1977, 1995 by The Lockman Foundation. Used by permission. (www.Lockman.org)

Copyright © 2014 by Elizabeth A. Nixon, Esq.
All rights reserved

Cover design by Justin Evans
Design Director: Bill Johnson

Visit the author's website at www.whitequillmedia.com.

Library of Congress Cataloging-in-Publication Data:
Nixon, Elizabeth A.
  Inspired by the Psalms / Elizabeth A. Nixon, Esq. -- First edition.
    pages cm
  ISBN 978-1-62136-559-4 (trade paper) -- ISBN 978-1-62136-560-0 (e-book)
  1. Bible. Psalms--Criticism, interpretation, etc. I. Title.
  BS1430.52.N59 2014
  223'.206--dc23
                                        2013049170

While the author has made every effort to provide accurate telephone numbers and Internet addresses at the time of publication, neither the publisher nor the author assumes any responsibility for errors or for changes that occur after publication.

21 22 23 24 25 — 12 11 10 9 8

Printed in the United States of America

*This book is dedicated to my husband, Jon,
who has always believed in me,
and that has made all the difference.*

CONTENTS

Part 2
Decrees Inspired by Selected Hebrew Words From the Psalms

Part 3
Decrees Inspired by Psalm 24 to Influence
Culture for the Kingdom of Heaven

FOREWORD

I HAVE ALWAYS BELIEVED in the power of God-inspired proclamations and personally make decreeing the Word a daily discipline because of the great benefits I receive from doing so.

I remember when the Lord first spoke to me about the benefits of decrees. I was in a season where I was shut down emotionally and lacked inspiration. He spoke a clear word to my heart concerning the importance of making daily decrees of the Word of God in order to fortify and edify my spirit in that season.

For months I daily declared who I was in Christ and what I had in Him. I made bold statements based on the Scriptures, but I did not actually feel like, "I was the head and not the tail." I did not feel like, "I was the righteousness of God in Christ Jesus." I did not feel like, "I was more than a conqueror in Christ," yet the Word said that I was indeed all these things.

At that time in my life I made a quality decision to believe the Word of God more than my circumstances, more than my feelings or lack of them, and more than what any individual might say. Over the months of making daily decrees I found things shifting in my circumstances. The Word of God truly does not return void but accomplishes everything it is sent to do. The Word of God builds frameworks in the unseen realm that then manifest in the natural. Decrees are very powerful!

Elizabeth A. Nixon skillfully unpacks insights regarding decrees. As a respected attorney, Elizabeth is familiar with the legal authority behind decrees. You will love the revelation she unfolds. Your faith will increase, and you will be truly stirred to engage in proclaiming decrees of the Word. Don't be surprised if you find your life taking new turns that release greater realms of blessing and opportunity.

You will love this book! It is one you will want to keep in your library as a resource as well as in your Bible to use during your devotions. Be blessed as you enjoy this powerful tool. I have been.

—PATRICIA KING
WWW.XPMINISTRIES.COM

Introduction
WHAT ARE DECREES?

IN THE WORD we read about declarations, judgments, and decrees. These are not interchangeable words for the same thing. They are unique and distinct.

The word _declare_ comes from the Hebrew _achvah_ meaning "to make known" and "to set forth details and information." In the Old Testament it is used as "to give a full account of or an explanation for." So when we make declarations, we are making something known or making an account of something. There is a good practical example of this when you travel internationally because part of the customs and immigration card you fill out is the "Declaration." The customs agents ask you, "Do you have anything to declare?" What they are looking for is an account of the items you are traveling with, specifically if you have fruit or weapons or money that you need to "account for."

> Decrees are the vehicle through which truths in the spiritual realm become tangible realities in the natural realm.

The distinction is that when we make declarations in the spirit realm, we are making an announcement of the things we already possess, the things that we are carrying with us and are already enjoying. By contrast, "decrees" are the vehicle through which truths in the spiritual realm, which are not yet our everyday experience, become tangible realities in the natural realm.

The Hebrew word _mishpat_, or "judgment," refers to the specific act of deciding a case or controversy and the procedures for rendering vindication and justice. This is a legal reference, and we see it in our court system today. People take each other to court and ask the judge to issue a judgment. They are asking for the judge to make a decision on the facts and to render a decision, a judgment, as to the outcome. It also includes the process and procedure that the plaintiff, defendant, attorneys, witnesses, and the judge must follow in order to avoid a mistrial. We know from Scripture that God the Father sits as our judge and that there is a procedure for Him to render judgments in our favor, and that procedure begins with our repentance.

> *Decrees are a tool for the fulfillment of Matthew 6:10, where Jesus teaches us to pray "Thy kingdom come, thy will be done in earth as it is in heaven."*

By contrast, the word *decree* is a much different, much bigger word. Decrees are a tool for the fulfillment of Matthew 6:10, where in the Lord's Prayer Jesus teaches us to pray "Thy kingdom come, thy will be done in earth as it is in heaven."

DISCOVERING DECREES

I was first introduced to decrees when I was given a "decree for finance," but being unfamiliar with decrees, I was reading it without an expectation for anything to happen. What got my attention was when my finances began to radically change.

At first, the money I had seemed to go further than made sense. For instance, at the end of the month I had paid out more dollars while having more money left over than I should have had given the amount of income that had come in. It also seemed as though sales and discounts were following me everywhere—and not just for random things at the mall or in the grocery store, but also for the things and brands I actually wanted. This got my attention because up until then it seemed as though only the brands I do not buy were discounted but not the specific item or brand I wanted to buy. So when suddenly everything I wanted was cheaper, I began to take notice.

But what really had the biggest impact was when my whole work-life balance shifted. At the time I was managing my own boutique law firm in Los Angeles, California, and had recently shifted from working full-time to only part-time. My expectation was that my income would drop relative to the fewer number of hours I was working. I was also expecting my stress level to increase for two reasons. First, I would have less time to get work completed, and second, given I would be working fewer hours, I expected a drop in income. But what happened took me completely by surprise.

As I used this decree for finance, my income increased. I was working fewer hours, with fewer clients, but the value of my services and income increased. My stress level also went down and not just because of the increase in income but also because the nature of the client work, and the clients themselves became less stressful. For a legal practice this is not the norm: work less, stress less, make more!

Decrees had physically, emotionally, practically, and tangibly shifted my work, my finances, my peace—in fact, my whole my life.

I knew I was on to something. But being a lawyer brings occupational hazards. Lawyers have to be able to prove a case beyond a reasonable doubt—even to themselves. It is ingrained in us. It is just the way we think. Therefore, even for me to really grab a hold of decrees, I needed to fully understand them and how they work—beyond a reasonable doubt.

I began to study and research decrees, as if preparing a legal brief on decrees in order to understand them. That's another occupational hazard for lawyers. We are trained to look at nuances and definitions and the tiniest details. When lawyers read a law or a statute, they dissect it to the barest bones to determine: (1) What does it mean?

(2) Does it apply in this case or to my client? (3) What is the consequence of the application?

So when I come to scriptures in the Word, I can't help but read them the same way. What does a specific verse mean? What do the individual words mean? How does it apply to my life? What consequences are there? Another way of asking this question is, "Given the meaning of this verse and having determined that it applies to me, how ought my circumstances and behavior be affected?"

In order to answer these questions, and specifically in order to determine "What are decrees?," I looked for three things:

1. What is the definition of the word *decree*?

2. How do decrees work? (That is, how do they operate in a cause-effect way?)

3. Where is their precedent in the Bible?

What I found profoundly changed my life.

Defining the Word *Decree*

My research uncovered four meanings to the word *decree*. They are:

1. An English definition
2. A biblical definition
3. A Hebrew definition
4. A German definition

English definition

In the English language a *decree* is a statement of purpose, truth, or vision, but it is more than just an announcement. A decree carries the same level of authority as a law being enacted or an order being issued by a court. What does it mean to have the same level of authority as a court order? Consider this example: If a defendant is convicted of a crime and sentenced by the court to prison, can that defendant object to or ignore that prison sentence? No, of course not. Why? Because the authority of the court order is such that upon conviction he has no further say in the matter.

The same is true with decrees. When we decree God's provision and blessings over our lives, then anything purposed against our provision and blessing can have no further say in the matter! When we decree God's peace and unity in our family, then anything purposed against peace and unity has no valid objection or standing to come against us!

Biblical definition

A biblical decree is one and the same as the very purposes of God because it is rooted in the Word of God. Think about the weight that the will and purposes of God carry—that is the same level of authority and weight as the decrees we speak. This is why we must only use decrees based on God's Word. The Scriptures are a great safety net to guarantee that you speak the will and purposes of God as you decree things into your life.

There are so many great verses to decree over our lives—verses for health, blessing, peace, protection, etc. But there are circumstances where it can be hard to find a specific verse. For example, if you are considering a change in job, a sale of a home, or returning to school, there's likely no specific verse to decree over your life. There's no Scripture reference any of us can turn to that says, "[*Your name*], sell your house on this day for this amount and move to such-and-such city to attend the college there."

Moreover, given the weight and power of decrees, I do not encourage you to make decrees about these specifics but rather choose to decree the will and purposes of God over your life.

This is important because oftentimes we can get a specific vision of how we *want* things to be and get so focused on that that we miss what God is actually doing. It is not uncommon for the way God unfolds His plans to look very different from what we expect. And this is a serious point.

Consider the Israelites. They missed the Promised Land because it did not look the way they wanted it to or the way they expected it to. When giants were found to be in the land, the Israelites chose not to enter in (Num. 13). We do not want to miss our promised land because it doesn't look the way we expect it to.

Consider also the Jews in the New Testament who missed their Messiah because He did not look like or act the way they expected. These are serious missteps in history all because people had a certain expectation and were unable to see God's hand.

Using decrees based on our hope or expectation rather than the Word of God can create confusion for us the same way the Israelites and New Testament Jews missed His perfect plan.

By contrast, decreeing specific scriptural verses imparts and releases the power of His living Word into our lives and circumstances without creating confusion or blinding us to His ways. If we are in a time of transition and are waiting for direction from God, we may not be able to find a verse to tell us what university to go to or what city to move to, but we can decree the power of His presence, and when we are in His presence, it is hard to miss what He is doing. For example, here is a section of the decree inspired by Psalm 13, included later in this book:

> I decree that Jehovah has not forgotten me! Though He hid His face from Moses in the cleft of the rock, He rent the temple veil and welcomes me into His intimate place where I look upon His face, consider His gaze, and worship Him.

This decrees reminds us that God has not forgotten us and that while we may not see clearly the specifics of what He is doing, we can see Him, and from that place we can hear from Him and move in confidence as we follow Him. This is why I use and recommend this decree:

I decree the will and purposes of God over my life!

It may be generic, but it is powerful! Essentially this is what we are decreeing regardless of an underlying Scripture reference because God's will and purpose for your life is an abundant life, complete health, safety, security, peace, prosperity, and success. Regardless of the geography, the timing, or any other specific, decree His will and purposes, and you will find yourself exactly where you need to be.

Using decrees this way, we are less likely to be focused on a specific way God's plan will be presented to us such that we are more easily able to have eyes to see the how and what God is doing as He brings it to us.

Hebrew definition

The next definition of the word *decree* is the Hebrew definition, which says to decree is to divide, to cut in two, to cut off, to destroy, to separate, or exclude.

This Hebrew definition shows us another facet of what happens in the spiritual realm when we speak decrees. For example, when we decree "I am blessed" (inspired by Psalm 112:1), not only are we establishing the blessing, but according to the Hebrew definition of *decree*, we are also dividing ourselves away from anything purposed against our blessing; we are cutting off and destroying the plans of the enemy.

When we decree "My children are strong and full of integrity" (inspired by Psalm 112:2), we divide our children's strength from their weakness and set them apart from deception. When we decree their

integrity, we cut off and destroy dishonesty and unrighteousness from
their midst and from their hearts.

When we decree, "My home brims with wealth" (inspired by
Psalm 112:3), not only do we establish our wealth with the authority
of a court order, decreeing it with the same authority as the decreed
will and purpose of God, but also we cut off spirits of lack and destroy
poverty spirits.

The decrees we speak institute and establish the reign of the
kingdom of heaven and cut off forever the reign of the kingdom of
darkness.

German definition

The final definition comes from the German word for *decree*,
diktat, which means a harsh judgment, imposed on a defeated enemy
that cannot be opposed.

In terms of spiritual ramifications this means that when we speak
decrees, not only are we proclaiming them with the authority of a
court order, and creating our circumstances to be one and the same as
the very will and purposes of God, and separating and dividing ourselves from the plans of the
enemy, we are also making a
harsh judgment and imposing it
on our defeated enemy, *and* it
cannot be opposed!

> *Decrees are a tool by
> which our circumstances
> come into alignment
> and agreement with
> the Word of God.*

These dual ramifications of
decrees are what changed my
whole world. When we make
decrees, according to the Word of God, we:

- Speak God's blessing upon our lives
- Cause our circumstances to be changed so as to manifest heaven while the enemy suffers a judgment of defeat that he cannot oppose

DISTINGUISHING DECREES FROM POSITIVE AFFIRMATIONS

Decrees are a tool by which our circumstances come into alignment and agreement with the Word of God. Despite my excitement to see the changes in my finances, I still held serious reservations about decrees for one reason. During my tenure in Los Angeles I had become familiar with the culture, mind-set, and philosophy of positive affirmations. Even though positive affirmations are based in spiritual, even biblical principles, they deny the truth of the Judeo-Christian tenets. I was not comfortable getting involved with decrees if they in any way related to or were aligned with positive affirmations.

In case you're not familiar with positive affirmations, they are integral to the human potential movement, which is a philosophy that came into being in the 1960s and blends New Age spiritualism with the concept that everyone is able to access their inner human power source to live an exceptional life and even influence the course of the universe so as to draw to themselves everything they want or need.

People engaged in the human potential movement are often very spiritually minded. They accept certain biblical principles as true, and many spiritual verses are incorporated within their beliefs, which include positive affirmations, the law of attraction, and the law of intention. For believers it is important to draw a clear boundary between what is biblical and what is not so that we can activate biblical principles and promises, which in fact we are commanded by God to do.

The human potential movement, the laws of attraction and

intention, and positive affirmations blended with New Age mysticism have taken such a deep root in our Western culture over the past decade that they have actually triggered a crisis in true, biblical faith evidenced by the fact that it has become common to hear their pop-spiritual-culture phrases even in churches, from pulpits and among believers.

Manifesting positive affirmations vs. manifesting the kingdom of heaven

Therefore it is important to understand what they propose as the basis for manifesting our desires versus what the Word of God says as the basis for the manifestation of heaven on earth. The following will break down the philosophies, beliefs, and teachings of the human potential movement and will provide a clear contrast to what the Word of God teaches.

> *For believers it is important to draw a clear boundary between what is biblical and what is not so that we can activate biblical principles and promises, which in fact we are commanded by God to do.*

You might have heard reference to the law of attraction and the law of intention without realizing it. You have often likely heard people say "I'm just putting it out there" or "I'm putting it out to the universe."

Specifically the law of attraction is a metaphysical belief that "like attracts like." That is, positive thoughts/actions attract positive things while negative thoughts/actions attract negative things.

The law of attraction would tell you that if you think or say "I need more money," then that thought and those words will only continue to perpetuate the circumstances wherein you will always need more money. The law of attraction operating through your thoughts and words is actually causing the need for more money to continue to be attracted to you. Their direction then is to state "I have as much money as I need," which will then, as they assert, access your own inner human power source to cause your circumstances, in cooperation with the universe, to manifest as much money as you need.

Similarly the law of intention operates based on your inner and stated intention in any given circumstance. The concept is promoted by gurus such as Deepak Chopra, who wrote *The Seven Spiritual Laws of Success* and explains the law of intention this way: "Inherent in every intention and desire is the mechanics for its own fulfillment."*

These blended precepts of New Age spiritualism and human potential seek to teach you that you can have whatever it is you desire. It causes people to believe that they can not only control their lives but also actually influence and control the universe.

An in-depth study of these philosophies reveals that the belief of being able to control the universe from your own internal power source is really another way of teaching that all humans are gods.

The human potential movement teaches:

- You are the one able to control your own world.

- You are your own power source for the effectiveness of your positive affirmations.

Herein lies the fault of these teachings.

People fully engaged in positive affirmations adopt it as a lifestyle. Everything from the kind of watch they wear, to the kind of car they drive, to the neighborhood they live in says something about who they are as they seek to "put it out there." All these things are by specific design in order to attract the kind of success they desire. The

---

* Deepak Chopra, *The Seven Spiritual Laws of Success* (San Rafael, CA: Amber-Allen Publishing; Novato, CA: New World Library, 1994).

Rolex watch "puts it out there" that they are successful. The German-engineered car "puts it out there" that they are successful. The million-dollar home they live in "puts it out there" that they are millionaires, even if buying the Rolex, the car, and the home are sending them into bankruptcy.

These teachings not only assert that we are responsible for the positive that comes our way but also that we are responsible for the negative that comes our way.

The problem is that all of us, no exceptions, have down days. We all have days where we get the wind knocked out of our sails and we lose faith. On those days when we just can't seem to get it together or keep it together, then these philosophies claim that we are responsible for the negative things those thoughts and days must certainly attract.

On the cosmic-karma balance sheet of life it is impossible to know whether all your work to "keep it together" and just smile and stay positive has been enough to outweigh these weaker failing moments.

For the finance and banking professionals that I networked with in Los Angeles, how do they answer for failing stock markets and investments? Weren't they supposed to be controlling that or, at the very least, controlling their own universe so their own accounts remained unaffected?

The problem with positive affirmations, the law of intention, and the law of attraction is this: if we are our own power source for the effectiveness of what the universe sends our way, at some point it all becomes too much. Regardless of how much you "put it out there," your boss's bad mood or failing global finance markets cannot possibly be reacting to your own thoughts and emotions. To be your own power source to effect the universe to your personal advantage and benefit, as a moment-by-moment priority, is too much. Too much pressure. Too much stress.

This is exactly what begins the cycle of having to "fake it," and faking an attitude of being positive prevents you from being real and genuine.

In the end, the power of positive affirmations is just a bunch of hot air, and when you have a down or flat day, or when circumstances beyond your control begin shaking, then everything comes tumbling down.

Having said that, though, there are some people who have found success in this philosophy and some have found quite a lot of success—and that is because the principles are based on spiritual, scriptural truths. For example, Mark 9:23 says, "If you can believe, all things are possible to him who believes" (NKJV).

So the human potential movement is tapping into these biblical truths. But they are falling down because they are putting the focus on the individual as the source, the one who is in control, and to those involved in the human potential movement, this is a "way that seems right" but in the same way that Proverbs 14:12 speaks of: "There is a way that seems right to a man, but in the end it leads to death" (NIV).

In the end, the human potential movement and related New Age philosophies all say that we are gods. This is the end that leads to death.

In fact, the word *way* in Proverbs 14:12 in its original Hebrew (*derek*) means, "the way of the fool" or "the way of self-indulgence."*

It would be correct then to read that verse this way, "There is a way that seems right to a fool, there is a way of self-indulgence that seems right, but its end is death."

The difference between those involved in the human potential movement and what the Scriptures say is basically where we place our belief, or in whom we have faith. The law of attraction, intention, and positive affirmations teach that ultimately you are a god able to

* Sacred-texts.com, "Proverbs Chapter 14," http://www.sacred-texts.com /bib/cmt/barnes/pro014.htm (accessed November 1, 2013).

control the universe and that you are your own power source for the effectiveness of what you achieve. There is no one else able to help you or to intervene for you or to work on your behalf.

So what is the difference in the Bible? Where should a believer look for the source of power to their faith?

Hebrews 11:1 reassures us with this: "Faith is the assurance of things hoped for, the conviction of things unseen" (NAS), but not based on some metaphysical world we are supposed to try and control all by ourselves, but rather on this truth from Hebrews: that God is, and that He administers His kingdom with love and mercy.

THE REAL POWER SOURCE FOR DECREES

While the human potential movement and New Age spiritualism place each individual at the center as their own power source, as the only one able to control or influence the outcome of their own personal desires and destinies, believers have a much stronger influencer working 24/7 on their personal behalf.

Two verses provide clear distinction for the difference between how positive affirmations work and where the power source for decrees lie.

Jeremiah 1:12

In Jeremiah 1:12 the Lord is speaking to the prophet Jeremiah, and He says:

> For I am alert and active, watching over My word to perform it.
>
> —AMP

This clearly establishes that the power source for manifesting promises from the Scriptures is not us, it is not the individual, but rather it is God. God in this reference is Almighty God. Jehovah. The Creator. The source of life, health, strength, provision, protection, abundance, and success. And this is another reason I recommend decrees from the Word of God, because as we are told here in Jeremiah, God Himself is active and alert—watching over His own Word, ready to perform it.

When we make decrees, it is not us changing anything. We do not have to will some great universal void to move or change direction or do anything. That is too big for us.

The benefit, beauty, and simplicity of decrees is that by speaking them, we are not seeking to move the universe; we are moving only ourselves. We are causing our own hearts, minds, dreams, visions, and emotions to come into alignment and agreement with God's Word. When we speak decrees out loud, we are putting a voice to them, and then God Himself is alert, meaning He is watching, looking, and waiting for someone to activate a promise by speaking it and coming into agreement with it. When we do, He is alert, meaning He is active and ready to put those words and promises into action.

When we put voice to His Word, that is when we come into agreement with Him and His Word, then He performs it for us! We agree with God's Word, we speak it, we activate it, He performs it.

Psalm 103:20

The second verse from Psalm 103:20 reads:

> Bless the LORD, you His angels, mighty in strength, who perform His word, obeying the voice of His word.
>
> —NAS

Angels have been given a direction from God to obey the voice of His Word. So when we decree the Scriptures, the angels are being released to do the work of His Word!

These two verses take all the pressure off us! We do not have to be responsible for every negative thought that races through our minds. We are not responsible for the course of global finance markets. We are responsible simply to read and agree with the Word of God.

When we do that, two things happen: both the angels and Jehovah Himself are released to perform the work and Word.

To clarify, we are not releasing or commanding God and His angels like some genies in an ancient, mystical bottle. Rather, God has already established life, joy, peace, health, unity, harmony, abundance, prosperity, success, vindication, justice (and the list could go on). God has established them for us. His angels have been assigned to carry out the necessary steps for them to be manifest as our reality. Decrees recite truth according to God's Word and thereby tap into the infinite power of the glory of God.

All we do is, finally, come into agreement with God's Word, which is the angels' and Jehovah's green light to do what it is they have been waiting all our lives to do. So while positive affirmations recite a self-generated, self-focused desire and assert to create it by tapping into the power of the feeble human sub-conscious mind, decrees recite truth according to God's Word, which, as Philippians 4:19 says, taps into the infinite power of the glory of God.

> *The benefit, beauty, and simplicity of decrees is that by speaking them, we are not seeking to move the universe; we are moving only ourselves.*

> God will provide all of my needs according to the riches of His glory, which are ours in Christ Jesus.
>
> —PHILIPPIANS 4:19, DARBY

Another powerful aspect of decreeing from God's Word is that when God's Word is spoken, it is impossible for it to just fall flat and not effect radical change. Isaiah 55:11 tells us that God's Word does not return void. In the Hebrew this phrase, "not return void," has a vastly greater meaning than we may realize. Here is that verse spelled out fully according to the original Hebrew language:

> So shall my Word not be revoked
> Nor shall it return to me void of fruitful works.
> No, for it shall accompany you
>   with many gifts of gold and silver.
> It shall produce, cause, effect, attend to,
>   put into order, observe, celebrate, appoint,
>   ordain and institute whatever I have pleasure in,
>   and in whatever I delight,
>   AND it shall prosper, advance, cause success
>   and make profitable whatever I (God) put my hand to,
>   all that which I (God) loose and send out.

That's what it means for God's Word not to return void. This is the effect you are coming into agreement with when you put a voice to God's Word and decree with the authority of a court order and cut off and separate anything set against it!

Activating God's Promises in Your Life

There are many promises in God's Word—promises for peace, security, health, prosperity, justice…the list could go on and on. But for many of us, the truth of these promises is not our daily experience. There are sadly too few who can say that peace, security, health, prosperity, and justice are all their day-to-day norm. Why is that? Quite simply the answer is often because we are yet to activate those promises.

There is often a general attitude that if a promise is written in the Bible, then it is for me and that it is automatically available to me. It should "just happen" or it should "just be." However, we see a clear example of needing to "activate" a promise before being able to avail ourselves of that promise in the promise of salvation. Romans 10:9 instructs us as follows: "If you confess with your mouth Jesus as LORD, and believe in your heart that God raised Him from the dead, you will be saved" (NAS).

In order to participate in, to receive, to have the benefit of, to actually be saved, there is a detailed instruction on what to do. First, confess with your mouth, and second, believe in your heart. Confessing and believing are the activators of this promise. If it were *not* necessary to "activate" the promise of salvation, then everyone everywhere would go to heaven—automatically—without having to "be saved." However, we understand from the Scriptures that this is not true. Therefore, we also know that this promise of salvation must be activated, and it is activated by confessing with our mouths and believing in our hearts.

Likewise, the other promises of God's Word can be activated by confessing and believing. The Greek word in Romans 10:9 for *confess* means to speak and to agree with or assent. This is exactly what we do when we decree. We speak it out, and we agree with the promise. We believe it is true, we believe it is true for us, and we believe it is for us for right now. When we decree God's Word, we are activating His promises.

> *Decrees recite truth according to God's Word and thereby tap into the infinite power of the glory of God.*

BIBLICAL PRECEDENT FOR DECREES

As I was putting all of this information together, I was obviously very encouraged. I was gaining confidence in decrees, but there were a couple of things that I still needed to check off my list, and one of them was the biblical precedent. Here again is that lawyerly occupational hazard—the need for a precedent. Where in the Bible are we taught about decrees? This is very important to me because the Scriptures must be the basis and foundation, so to find decrees being used and modeled was important.

The first precedent for decrees I found in the Word was in Job 22:28:

> Thou shalt also decree a thing, and it shall be established unto thee; and the light shall shine upon thy ways.
>
> —KJ21

As a lawyer, what I like about this verse is the use of the word *shall* because it has legal connotations. For example, if I am writing a contract for a client and I want to indicate that a certain action is optional, then I would use language such as "he can" or "he may," but if I want to make sure that a certain action is required, then I would use "it shall" because that indicates that it is mandatory and cannot be avoided or ignored.

In this verse the use of the word *shall* is where I had an "aha" moment. Job 22:28 is not telling us that decrees are a good idea or generally just a clever practice. Because of the use of the word *shall* we are actually being instructed, required, and commanded to decree.

That changes everything, doesn't it? This is not just the latest and greatest new tool: "Decrees—the next trendy thing in church." No. Decrees are required of us by God, and they come with a great promise. It's not that we are making decrees and crossing our fingers, hoping our wishes come true. God promises us that when we do, those things "shall be established." Again, see the significance of that word. He's promising us and making it mandatory in the spiritual heavenly realm, that when we decree a thing, it shall be established.

And just on a side note, while the meaning of the word *establish* is what we would expect—it means to fulfill, confirm, or impose certain conditions—it also means "rebuilding" in relation to ruins.

I like this because there were some areas of my life that felt as if they were in ruin or close to it. This verse encouraged me, saying that if I decree over those areas of my life and call them into alignment and agreement with the Word of God, then those things shall be established—they shall be rebuilt!

And then here is the last aspect of this verse from Job. The last section reads, "And the light shall shine upon thy ways." This verse is not talking about sunlight; it is not saying that it will just be a "bright, shiny, happy day." In Hebrew, this word is weighty and means all of these things.

When we decree a thing, it is established and rebuilt for us, then the...

- ◆ Light of God's life
- ◆ Light of His instruction
- ◆ Light of His prosperity
- ◆ Light of His presence
- ◆ Light of truth
- ◆ Light of righteousness
- ◆ Light of His justice

...will shine, illuminate, clarify, and direct our moral character. It will make us beautiful and bring happiness to our lives.

The second verse I found in looking for a biblical precedent was Psalm 2:7: "I will surely tell of the decree of the LORD: He said to me, 'You are My Son, today I have begotten you'" (NAS). This verse from the Psalms is most likely written about King David, and we know it was also a picture of the Messiah. But regardless of whom this was written about, what we do see is that this is a decree of the Lord. The Lord has made a decree.

This is significant because of Ephesians 5:1, which tells us that we are to be "imitators of God" (NAS). So if God has made a decree, and if we are to be imitators of Him, then we should be decreeing also.

The third and final set of verses I came across in looking for biblical precedent for decrees was Psalm 23—the very famous "The Lord is my Shepherd" chapter. As I was reading through it, I realized that it is actually written in decree form. Read this psalm now with a new perspective, and receive it as a fresh decree over your life:

> The LORD *is* my shepherd,
> I shall *not* want.
> He makes me lie down in green pastures;
> He leads me beside quiet waters.
> He restores my soul;
> He guides me in the paths of righteousness
> For His name's sake.
> Even though I walk through the valley of the shadow of
>   death,
> I fear *no* evil, for You *are* with me;
> Your rod and Your staff, they comfort me.
> You prepare a table before me in the presence of my
>   enemies;
> You have anointed my head with oil;
> My cup overflows.
> Surely goodness and lovingkindness will follow me all the
>   days of my life
> And I *will* dwell in the house of the LORD forever.
>
> —NAS, EMPHASIS ADDED

When we speak decrees, we are creating an open heaven, and heaven comes down to earth. This means that the truths of heaven become our natural experience and reality on earth. The purpose of decreeing God's truth over our lives is to manifest God's will for us from heaven to earth.

Interestingly, the biblical phrase "kingdom of heaven" or "kingdom of God" in passages such as Matthew 6:10 and Mark 1:15 could also be translated as the "sphere of God's rule." It is that realm where God's ways of doing things happen.

The tense of the Greek also depicts it as a present realm and not a future kingdom. This is revolutionary for believers. For too long the belief has been that all of God's promises become our truth only when we die and go to heaven. For example, in heaven there are no more tears and no more sickness; in heaven we will have justice. By stark contrast, the original Greek language shows us that God's realm is present tense. The promises of God are available now. This is why Jesus taught us to pray "Thy kingdom come. Thy will be done in earth, as it is in heaven" (Matt. 6:10). God's promises, plans, and purposes are all for us *now*.

This is confirmed in Matthew 10:7, where in commissioning His disciples Jesus tells them, "As ye go, preach, saying, The kingdom of heaven *is at hand*" (emphasis added). This phrase "is at hand" is from the Greek word *eggizo*, which means to bring near or to join. Jesus is announcing that His kingdom is (present tense) brought near or joined to us when we come into relationship with God. Therefore, all the benefits of being in Christ are not just available in heaven; they are also available to us now and are, in fact, already joined to those who believe in Him.

The purpose and power of decrees then is to see God's kingdom manifest in our lives as it is in heaven. Decrees, based on the Word of God, call us into alignment and agreement with Him and will thereby:

1. Renew your mind
2. Change your atmosphere
3. Bring heaven to earth

This is the power of decrees.

RENEW YOUR MIND

We find in Romans 12:2 that we are to be "transformed by the renewing of your mind" (NAS). When you decree God's Word, you are speaking truth, and truth will correct your thinking. For example, you may be feeling discouraged, but when you stand up and decree aloud with your voice, "No weapon formed against [me] shall prosper" (Isa. 54:17, NKJV), there is a visceral effect in the spiritual realm, much like lightning in the storm clouds.

Those words rip apart the dark clouds of the enemy's oppression. They set you apart for victory and impose irrevocable defeat upon your enemy. The truth sparks your mind to think correctly. The decree inspired by Psalm 148:13 is great when others have a way of getting you down and you need to reset your own thinking:

My life, character, and integrity shine brilliantly
Because He is the source of all that I am.

Even if I look foolish to other people, I don't care!
Enjoying the experience of His presence is too much to
   contain.

Who He is, exceeds any thought my mortal mind can
   conjure,

His realm is inaccessibly high and yet, He dwells within
   my heart.

He is and is the source of safety, riches, security and
   prosperity.
There is no enemy who can jeopardize His reign.

He is beauty. He is freshness. He is newness.
He is brilliance. He is brightness. He is light. He is and
   He is mine.

CHANGE THE ATMOSPHERE

Not only do decrees renew our own minds, but also they literally
change the atmosphere around us and have the ability to affect the
people we work with, the grocery stores we shop at, the roads we
travel on, and the homes we live in.

It may be hard to initially grasp the impact decrees have on the
atmosphere, but we have all experienced the atmospheric affect that
negativity can produce. How many of us have walked into a room
where another couple are and without hearing or knowing any of their
conversation or any of the circumstances, you have an instant knowing
that it is not good, that a fight is lingering, and that you want to get
out of there as soon as possible.

In the same way that negative words spoken into an atmosphere
can have a literal and physical effect, so too can the positive power of
decrees affect the atmosphere around us.

BRING HEAVEN TO EARTH

Decrees from Scriptures say things such as "I am blessed, and I walk
in prosperity." However, you may look at your circumstances and say,
"But I am not actually walking in prosperity." You may wonder, "Is it

a lie or is it wishful thinking or is it some kind of self-delusion to be decreeing things that you are not really experiencing?"

This is when we need to understand the role and purpose of decrees. Decrees are a tool by which we manifest the promises of God from the heavenly realm into the natural, earthly realm so that they do become our reality.

In Matthew 6:10 we are taught in the Lord's Prayer to pray, "Thy kingdom come. Thy will be done in earth, as it is in heaven." When we make decrees, we are aligning ourselves with and agreeing with the kingdom of heaven and commanding it to come.

Our circumstances may say "paycheck to paycheck," but the truth in the Word of God is that He provides our needs according to His riches in glory (Phil. 4:19). So when you are paying your bills and you seem to keep coming up short, decree over your bills and checkbook, "He provides all of my needs according to His riches in glory!"

The following is a decree inspired by Philippians 4:19, which was written incorporating all of the nuances of the original Greek:

> But my God, *shall*, is required to, has made it mandatory upon Himself, to fill the gap, to meet my need, to supply liberally, to cause to thrive, flourish, and proliferate, and to bring into reality everything that I need for my journey, according to His riches, wealth, and abundance of external possessions, His excellence, majesty, and absolute perfection.

Decree that verse before you begin paying your bills. Decree that verse when you fill up your car with gas. Decree that verse when you tip your waiter or pizza delivery guy—generously. Decree that verse when your washing machine breaks down—again.

Your mind will become so quickened with the spirit of God and His spirit of truth, it will be renewed so radically and completely that it will be hard for you to remember why you couldn't believe in His provision before.

You will also so charge the atmosphere with truth that you will create an open heaven. This open heaven portal will follow you and expand to your entire sphere of influence, affecting the people around you.

When you carry this open heaven atmosphere with you everywhere, even your workplace will begin to change. If the business you have been working for is failing, change it simply by bringing your renewed mind and the portal to the kingdom of heaven. That is the power of decrees!

- Decrees are bold statements of truth, vision, and purpose.

- Decrees carry the authority of a court order so that anything opposed to the truth decreed has no further say.

- Decrees separate, divide, and set you apart for the kingdom of heaven.

- Decrees cut off and destroy anything purposed against you.

- Decrees cut off and destroy anything purposed against God's blessing for you.

- Decrees impose an irrefutable defeat upon the enemy.

- Decrees renew your mind.

- Decrees change your atmosphere.

- Decrees create an open heaven that will go with you everywhere.

- Decrees will propel you into your destiny!

GET INTO ALIGNMENT

I also encourage you to start each day with a spiritual alignment. I have been doing this simple alignment exercise for years.

Just as in fertile soil all the proper elements provide the right environment for peak fruitfulness, so does the proper alignment of our spirit, soul, and body provide the best environment for peak fruitfulness of the words we speak.

Here is the simple exercise I use:

> *I speak to my spirit: arise, take your proper position. Lead me as head of my being, submitted only to the Holy Spirit. I speak to my soul—my mind, my will, and my emotions—submit to my spirit, submitted to the Holy Spirit, in proper kingdom alignment. I speak to my body: submit to my spirit, submitted to the Holy Spirit, in proper kingdom health and alignment, in the name of Jesus.*

Whenever I do this, I can actually feel a physical and spiritual shift. It's awesome.

DO IT! LIVE IT! BE IT!

The following pages contain decrees inspired by select psalms. Read them aloud. Command them over your life and over the lives of those in your household. Claim them for your businesses and your entire sphere of influence.

As you do, you will:

1. Order God's purposes and promises over yourself with the authority of a court order.
2. Speak with the knowledge that the enemy is being cut off and his plans are being ripped off your life.

3. Renew your mind with the truth about the presence and influence of God in your daily life.
4. Watch the kingdom of God manifest in your heart, your home, and your life, for this is our truest prayer: "Thy kingdom come. Thy will be done in earth, as it is in heaven."

Part 1

Decrees Inspired by the Psalms

THE JOURNEY TO writing these decrees began very simply. I had established the biblical precedent for decrees, I had clarified the boundary between biblical decrees and positive affirmations, and I knew I wanted to decree the Word of God. However, as I began searching the Bible for verses that addressed specific areas of needs in my life (peace, health, financial freedom, spiritual victory, business success, etc.), I also began studying the original Hebrew language. I was shocked by how much more revelation there was when I looked beyond the English translation. Too often the English words cut short the depth conveyed in the original Hebrew.

For example, in Psalm 40:1 it is written, "He inclined unto me and heard my cry." That is a beautiful picture in English. But there is deeper meaning to the words *inclined* and *heard* that remains hidden from the reader. In the decree inspired by Psalm 40:1–4, I have used the complete meaning from the Hebrew to allow us to decree the fullest revelation of this verse. This is what it fully means for Jehovah to "incline and hear our cry":

> *May you begin to see "His kingdom come in earth, as it is in heaven."*

At any moment Jehovah will break through! He is inclined to move on my behalf. In fact, it is His intention to do so!

With attentive, concentrated interest, Jehovah hears

29

and agrees with me! He consents to my petition and grants my request!

Jehovah has elevated me, increased me, and caused me to overcome! He raises me into His flow of strength and security.

The following decrees are the result of my research into each of these psalms and the understanding gleaned from studying the original Hebrew language. Each passage reveals a powerful, encouraging, and life-changing decree.

As you decree, watch your life transform. You will activate and access that realm of God such that Matthew 10:6 will become a reality in your life and you will begin to see "His kingdom come in earth, as it is in heaven."

1

I AM BLESSED
(Psalm 1)

I DECREE that I am blessed!

I am blessed when I walk, when I stand, and when I sit down. I am blessed when I am about my work, when I take a moment to pause, and when I put my feet up to rest.

I am blessed when I am about my work because I do not plan my ways according to the counsel of the wicked. When I pause to contemplate, I do not think about the ways of sin or consider its fruit beneficial. When I rest, I do not let my mind wander to sarcasm or making fun of others.

Instead, I walk in the ways of the Lord, governed by the fruit of His Spirit. I sit and contemplate the ways of godliness and relax in love.

My delight is in the guiding ways and instruction of the Lord, and in His law I meditate both day and night.

I am like a tree planted firmly by streams of water. I am strong and well fed. I yield my fruit in season. My businesses do not fail, and I do not suffer miscarriage in health or in justice. My leaves do not wither but are healthy year round.

I prosper in all that I do.

The Lord knows my ways, for my ways are His ways. I am the righteousness of Christ. I will never perish, nor will my descendants or our inheritance.

2

HEAVENLY PERSPECTIVE
(Psalm 2)

I DECREE:

God is my Father. I am His heir.

He sits in the heavenlies, at peace, His enemy conquered.

I am seated with Christ in the heavenlies, at peace, my enemies conquered.

I keep this mind-set and heavenly perspective throughout my day.

God sits in the heavens and laughs!

He laughs at the antics of His conquered enemies, because they are powerless before Him.

I sit with Him, confident in Him, and laugh at my enemies.

When the day seems set against me—not enough time, not enough sleep, I laugh.

The joy of the Lord is my strength.

When those I work with get into confusion and miscommunication, I laugh.

The favor of the Lord is my shield.

When my home is in uproar and emotions are raging, I laugh.

The love of the Lord covers a multitude of sins.

My way is sure and my path is clear because God's reign cannot be shaken.

God's plans for me are set—like the potter who molds the clay and kilns it so that it sets and is firm—so is my life molded by Him, set and burning with the fire of His presence.

My heart is full of wonder for my God, whose enemies have been broken by Him.

I meditate on His might and His power and am filled with holy reverence for Him.

My whole being shakes with joy and fear mixed together, as I contemplate His holiness.

With this God I am safe and secure.

With this God I can laugh at whatever comes my way.

My breath is the very breath of the living God.

3

VICTORY!
(Psalm 3)

I DECREE:

I am protected. I am surrounded. Jehovah holds my shield. Jehovah is my shield.

My head is lifted up above all my troubles. I look down upon all the activities of my day and see that they are ordered. Peace fills my soul.

I do not have to worry about defending my own name. My reputation and dignity are kept safely in Jehovah-Kavod, who is the God of all glory. My glory and my honor belong entirely to Him.

All my prayers, cries, and concerns are heard by Him. All my prayers, cries, and concerns are answered by Him. He is faithful to me.

Those who are set against me are of no consequence to me! I have no fear of them. The Lord sustains me. I am revived and refreshed just by declaring His name.

Salvation, deliverance, welfare, prosperity, blessing, peace, and victory, they have all been given to me as gifts from the Lord. They are mine. I enjoy and possess them in every moment of the day.

4

VINDICATION FROM THE LORD
(Psalm 7)

I DECREE:

The great thing about God is that I can trust Him. His eternal plan protects me, His friendship vindicates me, and His presence is my safe and calm retreat.

I am liberated from all the nonsense of the world's priorities. He alone is my goal. I pursue Him for no reason other than to enjoy Him.

Jehovah, I give you the highest place of my heart! You are established as the ruler over my family's generations. You are set above. I ratify your promises over my household.

The justice of the Lord wins every time. His justice is established over my life. The rights and privileges of the kingdom of heaven are mine.

Deliverance, victory, and prosperity are decreed for me. He has set them in place and established them. The time of breakthrough is now.

5

CROWN OF GLORY
(Psalm 8)

I DECREE:

God—Your name and renown are powerful in the earth!

But who am I that You give thought to me? Fashioned from nothing more than dirt and dust, yet You crown me with Your very own glory! You vest me with abundance, riches, and dignity.

God—Your name and renown are powerful in the earth!

6

AMAZED BY GOD!
(Psalm 9)

I DECREE:

I am amazed! I take great pride in the Lord! I sing praises to His name!

For He has maintained my just cause. Any situation arising against me is detoured far away before it reaches me.

Jehovah God abides forever. He is my stronghold. My trust is safe in Him. It is impossible for Him to forget me.

The eternal one is gracious to me. He lifts me up out of despair. I am set high above all others so I can declare His goodness.

I am amazed! I take great pride in the Lord! I sing praises to His name!

——7——
REWARDED FOREVER
(Psalm 10:16–18)

I DECREE:

From antiquity into eternity, from before all things until long after all things, Jehovah is. Jehovah is God. Jehovah reigns.

Nations and generations have come and gone, rulers and leaders have risen, but none have lasted; there are no others who stand the test of time.

Men with earthly ambition and greedy ploys are eradicated, but those without legal standing or means within themselves are vindicated forever and stand in judgment over their accusers.

While men of pride and vanity are disgraced by Him, those who are humble, who are long-suffering and kind, these He rewards with long life and the desires of their heart.

——8——
DELIVERED AND PROSPERED BY THE LORD
(Psalm 12:5–7)

I DECREE:

Now, at this very hour, Jehovah takes control!

For all the ways in which I have suffered sudden devastation, He takes my hand and lays waste to those who rail against me.

Now, in this very moment of time, Jehovah asserts His authority!

For all the ways in which I have been robbed and burgled, where my wealth has been ripped from my bloodline with violence, He sets things right and puts down those who trap and ensnare me.

Now, even as I speak, Jehovah stands in opposition to my enemies!

For all the ways I have been subject to oppression and abuse, He sets me upon a throne, safe from reproach and shame.

Now, even now, Jehovah stands and will remain to establish me!

For all the ways I have lamented, groaned, and cried for deliverance, He crowns me with victory and establishes my salvation and prosperity!

This is Jehovah's promise to me!

His words spoken over me are pure and straightforward. I can take them to the bank. He will perform them.

This is Jehovah's covenant with me!

This decree over me is clean and undiluted. He will preserve and protect me and mine from generation to generation forever.

9

HE HAS NOT FORGOTTEN ME!
(Psalm 13)

I DECREE that Jehovah has not forgotten me!

Though He hid His face from Moses in the cleft of the rock, He rent the temple veil and welcomes me into His intimate place where I look upon His face, consider His gaze, and worship Him.

I am not left to my own emotions, nor am I bereft of counsel. I do not have room in my heart for sorrow, for it is full of His presence. My enemies cannot exalt themselves over me for His foot is on their necks.

The Lord tends His gaze and regards me with delight. I am His great pursuit and His deepest pleasure. From before the foundations of the world He has had His eye on me.

His ears are trained to hear my cry. He waits and listens longingly for me. Not only does He hear, not only does He answer, but He also bestows His best. Jehovah's bountiful provision is rushed directly to my side.

The light of His countenance shifts the atmosphere around about me, establishing His ways, His justice, His faithfulness, His glory. My heart and my life shine in the radiance of His eternal, righteous delight.

Though the way is not always clear, I will never languish. My confidence is sure, my footsteps firm. The enemy trembles as I walk by. I am safe in His unshakable goodness. I am secure in His eternal hold.

He has persuaded me because of His divine mercy and unending favor. I am carefree in His loving-kindness, reckless in His joy and abandon. Jehovah alone is the source of my reward. Jehovah alone is my reward.

—————— **10** ——————

GODLY CHARACTER
(Psalm 15)

I DECREE:

I choose God's character as my own: integrity, righteousness, truth. These are like my backstage pass to God's personal tent. Because of them I can live with Him in holiness.

I take a stand against lies; I will not speak badly about others behind their backs, and I will not be critical of my friends. I choose to have soft eyes to see others. I have a soft heart and understand that they too are on their journey.

I fear the Lord and honor others who do the same. I am self-controlled and keep my emotions in check; I do not allow them to rule me. I am accountable for my actions and take responsibility for myself.

I am quick to be generous. I love to give to others and do not expect anything in return. I do not desire to profit from other people's loss.

Because I maintain a godly character, I will never be shaken.

—11—
The Ways of the Lord
(Psalm 19:2–9)

I decree:

The law of the Lord is perfect, converting my soul.

The instruction of the Lord is sound, refreshing my will.

The direction of the Lord is complete, leading my desire.

The ways of the Lord are full of integrity, restoring my character.

The testimony of the Lord is sure, making me wise though simple.

The witness of the Lord is reliable, making me astute though naïve.

The statutes of the Lord are right, rejoicing my heart.

The precepts of the Lord are just, strengthening my courage.

The principles of the Lord are straightforward, bringing joy to my heart.

The moral character of the Lord is upright, bringing peace to my conscience.

The principles of the Lord are pleasing, making glad my inner man.

The order of the Lord is fitting and proper, organizing my habits.

The commandment of the Lord is pure, enlightening my eyes.

The commission of the Lord is clear, illuminating my vision.

The directive of the Lord is impartial, managing my will.

The mandate of the Lord is sincere, lighting up my whole being.

The code of wisdom of the Lord is sound, reinforcing my mind.

The fear of the Lord is clean, enduring forever.

Respect of the Lord is moral, remaining into eternity.

Reverence for the Lord is ethical, continuing beyond time.

Piety before the Lord is appropriate, steadfast into perpetuity.

The judgments of the Lord are true and righteous altogether.

The justice of the Lord is divine, vindicating absolutely.

The privileges of the Lord continue, mending and making right.

The decisions of the Lord are just, saving all.
The Lord is God.

------ **12** ------

FULFILLING MY PURPOSE

(Psalm 20)

I DECREE:

The Lord hears my requests clearly and shouts His reply! Like a battle cry of victory from on high, the Lord declares His answer. I am exalted with Him because of His defense.

He sets me above in security; He sets me above in prosperity. In lofty places, beyond the reach of my worry, the Lord lifts me up and seats me with Himself.

In times of trouble, in the day and very hour of my cry, the Lord hears my voice and knows my name. His answer comes quickly, assuredly, and rings out from eternity.

His wisdom is like a sure handhold on a steep cliff ledge. His presence turns a narrow way into a wide, restful expanse; where there was turmoil now becomes a place of refreshing for my soul.

I am overcome. Trembling and vibrating deep in my being, the sheer force of His deliverance shifts realms, quaking spirit and soul.

His aid translates me to high places of salvation, prosperity, and victory!

The Lord grants me my truest heart's desire. His answer to my cry comes with perfect, complete abundance. Jehovah consecrates me in my purpose such that I cannot help but fulfill it.

13
WHAT A MYSTERY
(Psalm 21)

I DECREE:

Jehovah, the eternal One, the Creator, the One from the beginning, the One who has made it all possible, has withheld no good thing from me.

Words cannot put into proper expression the depth of my peace, nor am I able to fully describe the happiness, the joy that I have come to know.

What a wonder. What a mystery.

The size of His helping hand, the quickness of his aid, the sureness of His devotion, the truth that I am His delight is too big for me to understand.

His heart is for me. He purpose is—me.

For Jehovah has signed over the deed and the title to me. He has completed the gift and entrusted it to me; in fact, He has commanded to me the desires of my heart.

Stop and think about that.

14
THE LORD IS MY SHEPHERD
(Psalm 23)

I DECREE:

The Lord Jehovah is my shepherd. I shall not want for anything. He makes me rest and lie down in green pastures and wide open places.

He leads me beside quiet waters. His ways are calm, and they restore my soul. He guides me tenderly and gently upon paths of right thinking, right feeling, and right behaving.

Even though I walk through the valleys, through shadows and dark places, I have nothing to fear, and fear has no place in me, for the eternal One is with me.

His rod of authority and His guiding rod of protection console and comfort me, bringing me ease. In plain view of my enemies and those positioned against me—He lays out my defense and displays His weapons of victory.

The Lord Jehovah Himself anoints me. My mind, will, and emotions are flooded with His Spirit. His goodness and tender compassion pursue me, causing me to flourish in every season of my life.

I make my home within the inner, private chambers of Jehovah Himself

Within the security of His personal household—always.

—*15*—

AT HOME AND AT PEACE WITH THE LORD
(*Psalm 23*)

I DECREE:

The Lord, the Creator of all things, the divine One, He is my protector! He watches over me very carefully, with pleasure always in His eyes. Everything that I need is already in His hands, and He gives it to me lavishly! My cupboards never run low, my gas tank is always full, and I can tip generously. My spirits soar throughout the entire day. My heart is never heavy.

I live in a relaxed state, calm and confident. His rest is always new and fresh. In the midst of the day I can close my eyes and feel the coolness of His presence; He is my oasis.

When my mind is exhausted, He brings me back to my strongest self. When my patience is tried, He establishes His will in place of my own. When my integrity is tested, His ways always prove my character. Like currency at the exchange, I receive strength and vitality for my tiredness.

Even when my journey takes me through distress, danger, or dread, my thoughts and emotions are stable. I make absolutely no room for evil, misery, or distress, for the Lord Himself protects and avenges me.

His direction always leads me to safety.

The Lord establishes the details of my defense and extinguishes all arguments against me. He is the one to assess the value my life. Like the preparation of a royal banquet table, His care and attention to the details are focused for my benefit. The Lord straightens, orders, and organizes my life.

My head is anointed by the Lord. His anointing is blessings beyond compare. My whole life overflows with His presence and His goodness. His Spirit is life to me in all things. My home and life overflow so much, I am able to really enjoy sharing all that I have.

Goodness, favor, excellence, prosperity, happiness, kindness, grace, and beauty—they follow me and attend to me as my helpers throughout all my life.

I will remain and be at home with the Lord always. The Lord, the Creator of all things, the divine One, He is my protector!

—— 16 ——
THE EARTH IS THE LORD'S
(Psalm 24)

I DECREE:

The earth is the Lord's—the whole earth and all that it contains:

+ The continents with their nations, the nations with their peoples

+ The mountains with their caves, the caves with their treasures

+ The meadows with their trees, the trees with their fruit

+ The soil with its seeds, the seeds with their crops

The world is the Lord's—the entire sphere of creation and all it contains.

—— 17 ——
I TRUST IN THEE
(Psalm 25)

I DECREE:

I bring to You, Jehovah, the very deepest part of myself, the very essence of my life and breath, the most secret of my desires and hopes, I lift them to You—for You to bear and carry on my behalf.

I trust You. I dare to be confident and bold in my expectations from You. So secure in You am I, even to the point of recklessness, for You do not disappoint or put to shame.

I recognize how You operate and where You lead. Your skillful instructions keep me on track. I follow Your truth and freedom and am established. And so I walk in safety, victory, and prosperity.

You are ever mindful of compassion and tenderness, remembering those instead of the missteps of my early years. You water me with wise counsel and lay a foundation of intimacy. Your peace treaty of friendship is my safe place.

My desires, hopes, passions, dreams, and destiny are rich, growing, and prospering easily, blossoming with all good things. My life, my legacy, my posterity—we inherit all that You have promised.

—18—
TAKING MY INHERITANCE!
(Psalm 25:13)

THE ISRAELITES of old did it when they plundered the Egyptians and again when they took possession of their Promised Land.

I now follow suit, using their model as my license.

Those forces that have held me captive and in bondage, those in opposition to me that hold hostage my promise and inheritance, I decree over you:

- I plunder you!
- I dispossess you!
- You are expelled!
- I succeed in your place!
- I am now rich; you are destitute!
- I am now healed; you are broken!
- I now thrive; you are tormented!
- I now flourish; you are barren!
- I am full of life, zeal, power, and passion!
- The kingdoms, regions, nations, and lands are mine!

+ The wealth and secret treasuries give themselves over to me!

+ The power of His kingdom is in my hands!

———**19**———

CONFIDENT AND UNWAVERING
(Psalm 26)

I DECREE:

I live my life every day with integrity. I make my plans in faith with trust and expectation. I maneuver the course of each day relying on the Lord—confident, unwavering, and convinced that I will not fail.

I am not embarrassed to talk about the Lord. My voice and spirit ring true to all who hear the thanksgiving and gratitude in my heart. He has done extraordinary, amazing things.

Each step of my journey is established. The very soles of my feet are set on firm high places, and from the places of praise and great joy I declare blessing and adoration to the Lord.

———**20**———

COURAGE
(Psalm 27:13–14)

I DECREE:

If it were not for the reality that God is,
    if it were not for the truth of His faithfulness,
    if it were not for my confident assurance in Him,
It would be too easy to become discouraged.
But I do believe
    and I do know
    that I will see

the goodness of the Lord,
  now, in this lifetime!
Therefore, I wait—
  full of confident hope and expectation.
Therefore, I remain strong,
  telling my own heart and soul:
    Be full of courage!
For the One I wait on—He is faithful.
The One I wait on—He has promised it.
The One I wait on—He is coming.
I wait for You, Lord.

21

BLESS, ADORE, AND CELEBRATE HIM!
(Psalm 28:6–9)

I DECREE:

  I bless the Lord,
  I adore Him,
  I celebrate Him,
  And I bow before Him,
  Because He heard and answered my prayer!

  I bless the Lord,
  I adore Him,
  I celebrate Him
  I bow before Him.
  Because in Him I am full of hope and absolute confidence!

22

ALL THE GLORY
(Psalm 29)

I DECREE:

I ascribe to You, O Lord Jehovah, all the glory.
I give you the credit for all the wonders of the worlds.
I attribute to You majesty, might, power, and strength.

23

HOW GREAT IS YOUR GOODNESS
(Psalm 31)

I DECREE:

I trust the Lord. What a relief to know that I can. I trust in His ways, in His promises, and in His protection. Because I trust in Him, I will never be ashamed! I am delivered from my enemies. I am strong in righteousness.

The Lord listens closely and intently to me. The answers I need come quickly, without interference or misunderstanding. He takes time for me, there is no rush, I have all of His attention. I conduct my life so that He alone is the force and influence around me.

I reside inside the place of the Lord, in His temple, in His heart. There no gossip, anger, bitterness, lies, or revenge can reach me. My household is secure. My children are saved. Nothing that I own, or that is owed to me, can be taken from me.

Whatever the world tries to inflict on me is thwarted! The words of God, the power of His love, the steadiness of His character, they always provide a way for me, a way of escape and liberation. Truth opens up the path, peace shows me how to go.

I have adopted God's thoughts and ways as my own. With these as my tools for life, anything is possible! My abilities are limitless, my future is open before me, nothing can hold me back or press me down. Nothing!

——24——

FORGIVEN
(Psalm 32)

I DECREE:

I am absolutely privileged. I enjoy an advantage in life that others do not have: my sins are forgiven and covered! It's as if they were never even committed. I am humbled by the immense love that God has for me. His forgiveness transforms my heart and life.

I enjoy this forgiven status, this special class with exclusive benefits. Those who see the favor on my life are envious and are moved to seek God for themselves.

I am covered by the veil of God. He is careful with me, like a well-kept secret. Instead of trouble surrounding me, I am surrounded by songs of jubilant escape!

I am safe. I am delivered. I am secure. I am free. I pause to contemplate this truth.

My life is purposed for wisdom. All that I put my hand to is successful and prosperous. I am the apple of God's eye, and He never looks away from me.

I am transformed daily by the fresh mercy and gentle love of my Lord.

I am drunk with glee. I will not compromise my righteousness. My determination, passion, and courage are fixed because the Lord is mine.

—— 25 ——
THE BEST PATHWAY OF LIFE
(Psalm 32:8)

I DECREE:

The Lord guides me along the best pathway for my life. He advises me and watches over me.

The Spirit of God pays special attention to me. With prudence and judicious, vigilant care He imparts instruction and understanding to my mind. He imbues my spirit with His superior heavenly wisdom such that I am caused to have success and to prosper.

With the skillful precision of a master-teacher, the Spirit's accuracy points me in the right direction.

The strength of God establishes a firm foundation, and His vision waters the seeds of His promises within—such that His ways become my natural instincts.

Under the gentle and continuous gaze of His eyes I receive His deliberate counsel and kingly advice. His favor, approval, and partiality toward me pave the way for my every day and every circumstance—such that I am brought into the very best of everything.

—— 26 ——
I AM YOURS
(Psalm 34:1–8)

I DECREE:

I live my life bowed on my knees before You, God, my King.
I bless You. You are the Eternal One.
I praise Your character. I intimately know Your glory.

In the private place of my heart, I adore You.
In the public place of my life, I show my gratitude.
From the depths of my being, I brag about You.

I am not shy about letting my life be an advertisement for You!
I am an encouragement to others to find themselves in You.

I take great care in seeking You, and I know You take great joy
  in finding me.
You respond quickly to me and snatch me away from the
  enemy's ploys.
I have no fears. I am completely at peace.

I look to You. I am never ashamed.
Your light transforms my heart so I can smile.
I beam with pride and joy—I am Yours.

My mind and spirit are in total awe of You because I prosper
  in everything—everything that is ethical, excellent, and
  valuable.
My physical, social, and financial states always continue to get
  better and better!

27

EVERYTHING, ALWAYS
(Psalm 34:9)

I DECREE:

I love the Lord. I choose His kingdom.
I set myself apart from the world's ways.
I choose purity. I choose kindness. I choose being a good
  person.

I don't care if I look old-fashioned and boring.

I don't care if I am laughed at.

I fear God. I am in awe of His power. I am in awe of His humility.

Being snubbed by the world's system doesn't bother me at all.

Its definition of success is a façade, a complete fake.

The general attitude of having to "have it all" is empty and worthless.

I have more than the world can offer me anyway.

Poverty is afraid of me, and it runs away, escaping its own demise.

Lack and Need are terrified by what they see.

I live—completed.

Prosperity is mine, and it multiplies in my hands.

Happiness increases constantly and is infectious to all who cross my path.

My soul thrives, my intellect and understanding are limitless.

All this abundance, all this goodness, it has only one purpose in me

To reflect the truth and light of the holy One, my rock.

—*28*—

ALL THAT I LONG FOR
(Psalm 37)

I DECREE:

My trust is complete and satisfied in the Lord.

It is easy for me to think right thoughts and to choose suitable behavior.

I delight myself in the Lord, in the fullness of His majesty.
The attractions of the world have no influence over me.

I have committed every part of my day to Him.
I know I can trust God to bring me through successfully.
My reputation and credibility are protected and vindicated by
    God alone.
I cultivate my faithfulness with intention and purpose to know
    Him.

He gives me all that I long for:
The family I desire to have—children of strength, courage, and
    integrity
The home I safeguard—full of peace and laughter and joy
The walk with Him—resting under an open heaven.

I have inherited the land promised to me and to my ancestors.
I choose humility every day and wear it like a garment,
And it is like spiritual currency that affords me abundance and
    prosperity.
There is no room for anger, worry, or irritation in my heart.

My enemies are cut off, and the Lord laughs openly at them.
Their day has come for they have been conquered.
The weapons they formed against me have been shattered.
I see this truth and am encouraged by the provision the Lord
    has made for me.

I choose righteousness, and so the Lord sustains me.
My inheritance will stand forever.
I have no cause to be ashamed when opposition comes against
    me.
For when the world suffers loss, I enjoy His mercy and
    abundance.

I love justice and run to it like a lifelong friend.
I constantly look for ways to be gracious and kind.
I close my ears from gossip and turn my eyes from impurity.
My mouth speaks the kindness of His heart.

The Lord will never leave me.
My life and my household are forever in Him.

—29—
My Hope Is in You
(Psalm 38:15)

I decree:

My hope is in You! Not just fingers-crossed hoping without cause to believe. No!

I watch. I linger. I wait.

Expecting. Believing. Knowing.

You hear me! Not just like a noise in the breeze, without attention. No!

You listen. You respond. You answer.

Speaking. Singing. Blessing.

—30—
My Confident Hope and Expectation
(Psalm 38:15-22)

I decree:

My life is handed over to You, Jehovah.
The ruin I have made of it, the joke others have mocked,
I release control to You.

I come to You like a man goes to the exchange,
Like a man to the bank to exchange torn, destroyed currency,
I come to You to replace the broken with the new.

My confident hope and expectation is in You.

—— 31 ——
EXPECTING BREAKTHROUGH!
(Psalm 40:1–4)

I DECREE:

I am tying fast to Jehovah! Expectantly and eagerly, eyes peeled, ready.

For at any moment He will break through! He is inclined to move on my behalf. In fact, it is His intention to do so!

With attentive, concentrated interest, He hears and agrees with me! He consents to my petition and grants my request!

Jehovah has elevated me, increased me, and caused me to overcome! He raises me into His flow of strength and security.

I am powerfully established. My destiny is confirmed and ratified by God Himself, who is my refuge and confidence.

The Lord has arranged and settled my accounts, ensuring a flourishing success for me—whenever I take back any ground the enemy has trespassed upon!

A new resonance rises from deep in my soul. Fresh melodies pour continually out of my mouth. Never-before-sung psalms of joy declare His glory like never before!

—— 32 ——
IN YOUR FOOTSTEPS
(Psalm 40:8–13)

I DECREE:

I am in love with You, Lord! I am overjoyed, beyond-words thrilled to follow in Your footsteps.

I take great pleasure in bringing a smile to Your face, and I am filled with happiness to do what pleases Your heart.

Your instructions and advice are held deep in my soul. There is no better guidance than the principles of heaven.

You are my God, the God of truth and ethics. You alone measure out justice and salvation. You are the source and cause of my prosperity.

It is Your absolute delight and great pleasure to rescue me, satisfying and paying off my debts!

You plunder the enemy's camp, stripping him, snatching away from him any weapon or victory against me.

Quickly and without delay You step in, graciously and favorably rendering decisions in my favor. There is excitement in the angelic realms when You step in.

Your aid and assistance are brought swiftly and with joy.

You are in love with me!

—— 33 ——
VINDICATED BY GOD
(Psalm 43)

I DECREE:

Jehovah, the Eternal One, the One who is wisdom, knowledge, and understanding, the One who judges rightly, knowing the intents of the heart:

He vindicates me.

He silences the accusations against me.

He delivers me from lies.

His light of life, light of prosperity, and light of instruction guide me along the best pathway for my life.

His truth, faithfulness, and reliability lead me into correct thinking, correct feeling, and correct behaving.

The soundness and sincerity of His heart draw me up into His heights, filling my complete being with joy!

—— 34 ——

COMMAND VICTORY
(Psalm 44:4–8)

I DECREE:

In Jehovah, my King, success is destined for me!
Whether in private matters or in the public marketplace
Angelic delegations set in place what God has decreed.

In Jehovah, my King, liberation is already won for me!
Whether in matters of health, finance, or family peace
God Himself raises His voice to command my victory.

—— 35 ——

STANDING TALL
(Psalm 45)

I DECREE:

My heart is alive, I cannot even contain myself I am so full of life!

Words of praise come spilling out of my mouth, like water tumbling over the falls.

God has blessed me, deeply and truly, He has undeniably
  blessed me!
He has given me words like honey to speak to my friends.
He has given me a fragrance like jasmine to attract His grace.
Finally, I see myself as He sees me, and I am changed overnight.

I am standing tall, taller than I have ever stood.
Confidence is my new best friend.
I know no fear. I wear my armor with pride and with ease.

My sword is at my side, ready for striking.
My shield is raised and glistening in the light of His face
A breastplate of righteousness guards my heart.
Truth, of who I am, of my strength and victory, keeps me on
  course.

My enemies lay all around, defeated, beaten, and conquered.
They are at His feet, beneath His throne, silenced and still.
I stand before Him, covered by His blood, victorious.

I have a throne—it is His throne, glorious and pure.
I know the right way to live, and I am living my best life ever!
I love honesty, integrity, sincerity, and truth.
I put away drama and chaos and lies. I guard my peace.

The King has fallen head over heels in love with me.
He showers me with gifts day after day after day.
He has a procession of joy and laughter, and it surrounds me.

I set my mind toward the future, whatever it may hold.
My inheritance has been restored.
My children will fill the earth and carry on this legacy of love.
We will remember the Lord and His goodness for generations
  to come.

— 36 —
HIS GRACIOUSNESS
(Psalm 51)

I DECREE:

God, You are so gracious to me.

You pour out mercy upon me when I need it.

You lavish me with favor when I do not deserve it.

God, You are so gracious to me.

God, You are full of tenderness toward to me.

When I am full of shame, You stand by me with faithfulness.

When I am accused even by my own deeds, You reserve pity
   for me.

God, You are full of tenderness toward to me.

God, You sing songs of joy over me.

When the strength of my life falters, You breathe Your delight
   into me.

When I am crushed to pieces, Your spirit and strength restore
   me.

God, You sing songs of joy only and always over me.

— 37 —
MY SOURCE
(Psalm 52:8–9)

I DECREE:

You have made me like a green olive tree—growing, maturing,
   standing, fruiting, flourishing, residing in the very midst and
   depths of Your heart.

Therefore, I trust in Your loving-kindness. I will never have
cause to doubt You.

Therefore, I am forever grateful to You, because it is You who
has established me.

Therefore, I happily wait patiently for You, for You are my only
source of blessing.

——— *38* ———

BECAUSE OF YOU
(Psalm 54:6–7)

I DECREE:

Because of You
Whatever it costs,
Whatever it takes,
I do it happily.

Because of You
I am grateful,
Full of appreciation,
And that is how it should be.

Because of You
I look upon my life
With hopeful expectation
And great satisfaction.

—— *39* ——
RIGHT HAND
(Psalm 63:8)

I DECREE:

Your right hand extends toward me. You guide and direct me in the right direction. You keep me, according to Your Word, on the right path.

Christ is seated at the right hand of the Father. I am in Christ and remain with Him, at the right hand. The Father welcomes me to join Him and to sit at His right hand.

All of the Father's kingdom is at my right hand, within reach—full of aid and comfort, complete with victory and strength.

Victory, strength, honor, wealth, riches, and success—all of these are mine, they are in Your right hand. They are at my right hand.

—— *40* ——
HOW BLESSED
(Psalm 65:4)

I DECREE:

Wow! You, God, maker of the universe, have chosen me.

I have been tested, I have been searched.
I have been examined as through a microscope
And I have been found pure, spotless, shining.

You position Yourself above and around me.
You draw in close to hold and protect me.
Your embrace holds me gently and tenderly.

My excellence is high above all others
I have been selected as the preferred one.
My attributes bring the Lord joy and pleasure.

—— 41 ——
SHOUT! CRY OUT! CLAP!
(Psalm 66:2)

I DECREE:

I shout! I cry out! I clap my hands!
I raise my voice in victory!
I sing! I dance! I march!
I set high praise in its place.
I confer my affection on Him.
I direct my adoration upon the One.
I transform the atmosphere everywhere.
Publicly. Privately. Joyously. Boisterously.
I shout! I cry out! I clap my hands!
I raise my voice in victory!
I sing! I dance! I march!

—— 42 ——
INHABIT ME, OH LORD
(Psalm 66:8–13)

I DECREE:

I bless You, Lord.
I set this time aside specifically to remember You and all that
    You have done.
I make a point to tell others of Your faithfulness.
I am overwhelmed by You.

I am set in place by my Creator.

I have been painstakingly and carefully positioned exactly in
    this place.

I have authority over it, I rule over my household with the fear
    of the Lord.

He tolerates nothing that prevents or impedes my strength and
    stability.

I am sure in Him, in all things, in all places, in all
    circumstances.

I am refined as silver.

As beautiful, precious, perfect, pure, solid silver.

Like a lover who carefully washes his bride—bathing and
    making her beautiful; I have been prepared by the Lord.

I am prepared for my Lord to inhabit me as His dwelling place.

Inhabit me, O Lord. Completely and totally take me over.

The Lord has caused me to be brought into His castle, into His
    presence.

You, Lord, have brought about the pressure of labor pains,

I am the seat of all You have promised to bring to bear and to
    pass.

You have strengthened me there in that place of labor and have
    delivered me.

I am at peace—satisfied and complete in all that we have
    promised to each other: I am Yours and You are mine.

——*43*——
HIS FACE SHINES
(Psalm 67)

I DECREE:

> God is merciful to me.
> His grace surrounds me.
> His favor restores me.
> His face lights up with joy and shines upon my entire
>   household.

> The Lord shows me where to go.
> I recognize His voice when He speaks.
> I am directed by His moral character.
> His path leads me to safety, and in Him is my prosperity and
>   victory.

——*44*——
THE BARAK BLESSING OF THE LORD
(Psalm 67:7)

I DECREE the blessing of the Lord upon myself: favor, counsel, prosperity, happiness, abundance, healing, safety, instruction, protection.

I decree the blessing of the Lord upon my life: favor, counsel, prosperity, happiness, abundance, healing, safety, instruction, protection.

I decree the blessing of the Lord upon all my children: favor, counsel, prosperity, happiness, abundance, healing, safety, instruction, protection.

I decree the blessing of the Lord upon my home: favor, counsel, prosperity, happiness, abundance, healing, safety, instruction, protection.

I decree the blessing of the Lord upon my extended family: favor, counsel, prosperity, happiness, abundance, healing, safety, instruction, protection.

I decree the blessing of the Lord upon my inheritance: favor, counsel, prosperity, happiness, abundance, healing, safety, instruction, protection.

I decree the blessing of the Lord upon all my household: favor, counsel, prosperity, happiness, abundance, healing, safety, instruction, protection.

I decree the blessing of the Lord upon all my friends: favor, counsel, prosperity, happiness, abundance, healing, safety, instruction, protection.

I decree the blessing of the Lord upon all my businesses: favor, counsel, prosperity, happiness, abundance, healing, safety, instruction, protection.

I decree the blessing of the Lord upon all my investments: favor, counsel, prosperity, happiness, abundance, healing, safety, instruction, protection.

I decree the blessing of the Lord upon my debts and taxes and obligations: favor, counsel, prosperity, happiness, abundance, healing, safety, instruction, protection.

I decree the blessing of the Lord upon all my enemies: favor, counsel, prosperity, happiness, abundance, healing, safety, instruction, protection.

I decree the blessing of the Lord upon all those who are set against me: favor, counsel, prosperity, happiness, abundance, healing, safety, instruction, protection.

I decree the blessing of the Lord upon all my spheres of influence:

favor, counsel, prosperity, happiness, abundance, healing, safety, instruction, protection.

I decree the blessing of the Lord upon all those who cross my path: favor, counsel, prosperity, happiness, abundance, healing, safety, instruction, protection.

I decree the blessing of the Lord upon all my words: favor, counsel, prosperity, happiness, abundance, healing, safety, instruction, protection.

I decree the blessing of the Lord upon all my worship: favor, counsel, prosperity, happiness, abundance, healing, safety, instruction, protection.

I decree the blessing of the Lord upon all my praise: favor, counsel, prosperity, happiness, abundance, healing, safety, instruction, protection.

I decree the blessing of the Lord upon all my thoughts: favor, counsel, prosperity, happiness, abundance, healing, safety, instruction, protection.

I decree the blessing of the Lord upon my inner being: favor, counsel, prosperity, happiness, abundance, healing, safety, instruction, protection.

I decree the blessing of the Lord!

45

GOD BLESSES ME
(Psalm 67)

I DECREE:

Elohim, You have put on public display all Your gracious works toward me. You have published in the heavens all of Your favor reserved for me. Release now the fullness of Your blessing. Flood my spirit, soul, and body with Your presence. Illumine my path with the gaze of Your watchful eye. Imbue the fullness of my days with Your Spirit.

Cause Your way, Your direction, Your moral character, and Your course of life to be perceived and understood by all people and all lands to the ends of the earth.

Cause Your life, Your health, Your prosperity, and Your victory to reach all the peoples of the earth in all generations.

I praise You and am full of joy, for even the earth produces for my benefit, giving over all of its fruit, wealth, and riches.

And You, as my Holy Judge, render decisions in my favor.

You declare over me prosperity, healing, and abundance.

——— 46 ———

I RUN TO YOU!
(Psalm 71)

I DECREE:

Thank You, God! I can run to You for whatever it is that I need!

Safety, protection, and security—You are the rock I grab and hang on to.

Peace, calm, and quietness—You are the place I can rest.

Success, victory, and prosperity—You are the way to having it all.

You do what it is You do so well—and that gets me out of trouble!

You bend down low, with Your ears and eyes trained on me.

You lift me up, dust me off, and set me back on my feet on Your path.

——47——
STRENGTH IN ADVANCING YEARS
(Psalm 71:18, 21)

I DECREE:

"Old and gray" do not apply to me!
I may have many years under my belt,
And I may have different color hair than when I was a youth,
But my strength, valor, and vigor increase every year!

It's Your majesty and mystery that keep me vital and strong.
Like displaying the weak to confound the wise—
I am your aged warrior confounding the myth of youthful
    strength,
I am up with the sun, praying through the night, never tiring!

The only thing my seniority of years displays is Your higher
    ways.
I do not decrease or shrink or shy away from opportunities,
Rather You continue to increase my spheres of influence.
You raise my dignity and use my voice to sing Your praise!

——48——
AS A KING REIGNS
(Psalm 72)

I DECREE:

Jehovah, You haven't come to subject me under Your rule,
Rather You have raised me up to rule with You from Your
    throne.

You have given me Your ethics and Your strong moral character.

You have given me a heart to see with compassion and tenderness.

You have given me strength to govern consistently.

You have given me wisdom to discern a quarrel and out the oppressor.

You have entrusted me with those who have no voice of their own.

You have put in my jurisdiction those who have no legal standing.

You have appointed to me the impoverished who cannot afford help.

You have employed me to be the hope for those who have given up.

Jehovah, let us reign together from Your throne.
Justice. Vindication. Welfare. Peace.

—— 49 ——

THE LORD CONTINUES
(Psalm 72:8)

I DECREE:

You, O Lord, will outlast the reign of the sun.
You will outlive the orbiting seasons of the moon.

Through generation, age, and epoch,
Beyond kingdoms and empires,
You continue.

Your presence drifts toward me like a sea-blown mist.
Your fragrance floats around me like dew on cut grass.
Your laughter bursts like rain upon the spring blossom.

Your peace carries on past the ocean waves' reach
Your kingdom expands well beyond the rivers and rims of the
earth.

Through generation, age, and epoch,
Beyond kingdoms and empires
You are.

———— *50* ————

IT IS PERFECT WITH GOD
(Psalm 73:28)

I DECREE:

How perfect it is for me to go to God!

By coming in close, by moving nearer and nearer
I am purified and my moral character is enriched!

By approaching His throne and all the creatures,
I am in the company of joy and happiness.

By humbling myself and acknowledging Him,
I am caused to prosper in every good thing.

Jehovah is glad to be imposed upon!
He loves for me to put all my hopes in Him!

My trust is safely placed in His care.
He is my vindication from danger and deceit.

Jehovah is the artisan of artists!
His wealth and wonders speak a thousand words!

How perfect it is for me to be in God.

——51——
WITH A LOUD VOICE!
(Psalm 75:1)

I DECREE:

I am so grateful!
I am so thankful!
I say it with a loud voice.
I repeat myself over and over.
Who You are, O Lord—
The things that You do—
They amaze me.
They hold me enraptured.
I am unable to look away.
The words to explain the depths of You escape me.

——52——
PROMOTION AND ADVANCEMENT
(Psalm 75:6–7)

I DECREE:

It's not my job.
It's not my boss.
It's not my good idea.
It's not my own ability.
It is only, ever, always You who brings promotion.

Yours is the only approval I seek.
Yours is the only praise I need.
Yours is the only smile that I look for.
Yours is the only endorsement I desire.
It is only, ever, always You who brings advancement.

—— *53* ——
IN PRAISE
(Psalm 76:1)

I DECREE:

In praise, God is revealed.
In praise, God appears.
In praise, God makes Himself known.
In praise, God is experienced.
Therefore I will praise you always!

—— *54* ——
SELAH
(Psalm 76:9)

I DECREE:

God—the divine One, enthroned in the heavens—
Has stood up for me.

He stirred up the situation
And imposed Himself upon the outcome
In order that justice would be accomplished for me.
As the original, eternal, good judge,
He determined the sentence for those things set against me.

Stress, anxiety, illness, oppression, mental fatigue, exhaustion,
A lack of friends and compassion and understanding from
    others—
He has put it all to an end.
He has put an end to the immorality that surrounds me
And has clothed me in purity.

He has cut off the voices that speak lies to me and about me,
And has clothed me in truth and liberty.
He has taken the sickness that weakened and fatigued my soul
    and body
And has clothed me in strength and life.

Selah: I pause to be grateful.

God—the divine One, enthroned in the heavens—
Has stood up for me.

—— 55 ——

MINDFUL OF ALL GOD IS
(Psalm 77)

I DECREE:

When I am mindful of all that God has done for me,
When I am mindful of all that God has done through the ages
When I am mindful of all that God is…

I cannot question Him!
I cannot question His ways!
I cannot question His timing!

—— 56 ——

THE INTEGRITY OF HIS HEART
(Psalm 78:72)

I DECREE:

God watches over me,
Providing for me,
According to the integrity of His own heart.

God watches over me,
Leading and directing me,
According to the wisdom of His depths.

————**57**————
EXCEL AND SHINE
(Psalm 80:1)

I DECREE:

I excel in purity and
Shine with newness, as I
Contend for God's kingdom.
He is my best friend.

He compels unity in my midst and
Multiplies His favor toward me and
Gives to me daily without reservation.

————**58**————
JEHOVAH IS MY GOD
(Psalm 81:10)

I DECREE:

Jehovah, the eternal existing One, is my God!
He has picked me up and caused me to be carried above and
    away,
Leaving all torment and failure far behind.

Whenever I lift my empty hands up to His throne
And open my mouth for words to speak or sustenance to be
    filled,
He satisfies to overflowing every part of me that longs for Him.

——59——
JUST A GLIMPSE OF YOU
(Psalm 84)

I DECREE:

From the innermost place of myself,
I am determined to seek the Lord.
From the part of my soul that lies awake at night,
I crave His most intimate presence.
My heart, emotions, and even my physical body
Sing with joy, inviting the King to overcome me.

This new happiness I have found—
It is clean, washed from the waterfall of His joy.
It makes even my thoughts shine and be pure.

The strength of person and conviction
Released upon me from His high tower
Brings resilience and conquers all fear.

Even when I pass through seasons of tears,
They create a deep well of life within me—
A source of growth, life, and blessing

Because of this I know
That just a glimpse of Your goodness
Can last me a lifetime.

You are the light, powerful and immense,
Standing as a prince over His betrothed,
Defending me against the world, against time.

There is nothing that You will keep from me,
Nothing that You will withhold or take away.

It is Your favorite joy to bless me.

You signed the title over to me, life is mine to enjoy.
I am completely accepted and enjoyed by You.
Every day You are extravagant in Your gifts to me.

I can live in complete abandon toward You,
Completely unrestrained in my love and devotion for You,
Because I am that safe and secure in the place You've made
    for me.

——— 60 ———
YOU ALONE ARE GOD
(Psalm 86:1–10)

I DECREE:

Jehovah, I see You leaning in my direction—focused, listening.
I'm in a one-on-one audience with my Creator King.
You are moral, full of favor and mercy.
Your works are extraordinary and true.

Jehovah, I feel You embracing me—gracious and kind.
There are no other gods, none like You.
You hear, You listen, and You care.
You pour out an abundance of blessings upon me!

——— 61 ———
YOU TEACH ME YOUR WAYS
(Psalm 86:11–17)

I DECREE:

Jehovah walks with me along this path of life,
Directing me through the twists and turns,

Instructing me along the journey ahead,
Training me to go the distance.

As a result,

I live ethically, stable in all my ways.
I pursue a way of divine instruction,
Carried along, enjoying soundness of mind and
Perpetual fidelity.

——62——

Protection
(Psalm 91)

I decree:

Ah, to rest. To sit in the Lord's presence, to relax in His beauty, to trust His strength. This is how I spend my nights!

I declare that the Lord God, who is above all things, is my home base, my safe place. I remember the childhood games where "home" was the safe place and that no one could touch you while there. As I go through all the "games" of my day, I declare the Lord is my safe place. My trust and my confidence are absolute in Him.

I am rescued from surprises and protected from hazards. I am entirely safe because Jesus fends off all danger. When traffic is hectic, I am safe. When coworkers are devious, I am protected. Whether traps or dangers are known to me or not, I am confident and fear absolutely nothing.

Others may suffer, but I do not have to. I expect the complete favor of God because He holds nothing back from me. His love is not conditional. His protection extravagantly surrounds me. I cannot even be grazed by danger. It's as if I am watching from a long distance away where nothing can reach me. I am bold in my expectation of comfort, happiness, and security.

I declare that I am not intimidated.

The Lord Himself has ordered His angels to stand guard over me wherever I go. If I stumble, they will catch me because it is their job to keep me from harm. Angels, do your job.

I hang on to Jesus with everything I have. I know beyond the shadow of a doubt that He can and will get me out of any trouble. I receive the best possible care when I rest and trust Him completely.

Jehovah decrees over me, "Call me and I will answer you. I will rush to you and remain at your side through all the ups and downs. I'll celebrate you with festivities and give you a long life, a long drink of My provision."

So I call upon the Lord knowing that He has already answered me. Jesus has rushed to my side and remains with me through it all.

I am celebrated with festivals of pure joy. I enjoy my long, rich, full, blessed, and honored life. And so it will be forever.

—— 63 ——
WHERE ARE THE WORDS?
(Psalm 92)

I DECREE:

Where are the words?
How can letters and syllables contain the depth of my wonder
    for Your name?

Where are the words?
Feeble are the attempts of my mouth as it strains to express my
    heart.

I am happy. I am glad. I am thankful and grateful.
These things are true, they vibrate within my spirit, but they all
     fall short.

I sing. I play instruments. I dance, jump, and skip.
But how do I put on the outside this feeling that I have on the
     inside?

You are the Most High. You are the only true and living God.
Who am I to celebrate Your goodness, Your kindness, Your
     faithfulness?

You are steady, stable, and true, our reliable, unchanging
     security for eons.
How can I laud You appropriately and sufficiently?

Your purposes, plans, and intentions throughout the ages
Are profound and unsearchable, existing beyond our
     imaginations.
You cause me to flourish.
Your hand surrounds me with an abundance of every good
     thing.
I bloom and prosper, in season and out, increasing into
     greatness.

Even in old age, beyond the natural time of things,
I spontaneously burst forth, proliferating with increase and
     intensifying with life.

You make me full and rich and wealthy,
Substantial in strength, wisdom, and grace.

Where are the words?

——64——
WONDERFUL IS THE LORD
(Psalm 96:1–6)

I DECREE:

I call upon the minstrels to sing a brand-new song and inscribe
fresh poetic verse,
So that we may proclaim the amazing news of God's provision!

I lift up my voice with a loud shout, imploring the musicians to
strum and chorale choruses to sing in rounds,
So that we may make known the incredible news of God's
deliverance!

His salvation is forever.
His victory is already secure.
The flags are flying.
It is done!

His welfare is rich.
His prosperity overflows.
The accounts are full.
It is complete!

Such is the greatness of God—
The heavens display glory and majesty,
Yet they are merely a dim reflection
Of the true sanctuary where He dwells.

I call upon the minstrels to sing a brand-new song and inscribe
fresh poetic verse.
I lift up my voice with a loud shout, imploring the musicians to
strum and chorale choruses to sing in rounds
For such is the wonder and beauty and love of the Lord!

65

THE GLORY IS YOURS
(Psalm 96:7–13)

I DECREE:

The glory is Yours.
Let the heavens declare.

The strength is Yours.
Let the seas roar.

The reputation is Yours.
Let the trees sing.

The offerings are Yours.
Let the fields cry out.

The courts are Yours.
Let the creatures bow.

The worship is Yours.
Let the people rejoice.

66

I SEE YOU
(Psalm 98:1–3)

I DECREE:

I see You, Lord.
I see Your right hand.
I see Your holy arm.
I see Your extraordinary greatness.
I see Your miracles.
I see Your surpassing strength.

I see Your direction.
I see Your guiding hand.
I see Your victory.
I see Your salvation.
I see Your faithfulness.
I see Your success.
I see Your welfare.
I see Your prosperity.
I see Your protection.
I see Your readiness.
I see Your holiness.
I see Your sacredness.
I see Your deliverance.
I see Your opulence.
I see Your liberation.
I see Your help.
I see Your defense.
I see Your moral character.
I see Your valor.
I see Your virtue.
I see Your righteousness.
I see Your crown.
I see Your kingship.
I see Your lordship.
I see Your judicial robes.
I see Your judgment.
I see Your vindication.
I see Your truth.
I see Your fidelity.
I see Your steadfastness.
I see Your stability.

I see Your justice.
I see Your loving-kindness.
I see Your faithfulness.
I see Your goodness.
I see Your mercy.
I see Your zeal.
I see Your desire.
I see Your grace.
I see Your favor.
I see You, Lord.

—— **67** ——

The Lord Is Before Me
(Psalm 102)

I DECREE:

The Lord is ever before me. He hears my cry. He knows my
voice.

He listens for me with answers ready.

God reclines on His throne, in my heart, at home with me. The
cherubim attend to Him.

Their company, the angels, and the Lord, quietly bring rest to
my soul.

My days and my troubles, as difficult as they may seem, are
really just fleeting moments

Before the eternity of the Most High, whom I love and in whom
I am secure.

——68——
YOU HEAR ME!
(Psalm 102)

I DECREE:

You hear me!
You listen!
You turn Your face to me, and
You answer immediately.
You are too gracious to me, O Lord,
So gracious and full of mercy and kindness.
Surely You do live forever
And the season of Your favor knows no end.
My children and their children
Will be established in You forever.
This is why I love you so much:

You hear me!
You listen!
You turn Your face to me, and
You answer immediately.

——69——
NO GOOD THING WITHHELD
(Psalm 103:1–5)

I DECREE:

Yahweh, Jehovah, You have withheld no good thing from me.

The mistakes I have made,
You have corrected.

Where I was wrong and even chose to be cruel,
You have forgiven.

The sickness, disease, and oppression that take hold,
You have healed.

The pitfalls and dangers of life that lurk about to trap me,
You rescue me out of the very middle of it all.

What can I say and how often can I say it
To emphasize enough how grateful I am?

Yahweh, Jehovah, You have withheld no good thing from me.

When my stomach is empty,
You fill it with delicacies.

The ache in my heart,
You answer with Your love.

When anger and disputes arise around me,
You settle them with grace.

What can I say and how often can I say it
To emphasize enough how grateful I am?

Yahweh, Jehovah, You have withheld no good thing from me.

—— *70* ——

ON EARTH AS IT IS IN HEAVEN
(Psalm 103:19–22)

I DECREE:

Bless the Lord!
All angels who obey His word and serve His people
Praise and celebrate Him!

Bless the Lord!
All the works of His hands throughout all His creation—
Bless the Lord, oh, my soul!

71

THE LIGHT OF GOD
(Psalm 112:1–5)

I DECREE:

Jehovah's light upon my life guides me like the powerful
intensity of a lighthouse.
Like the brilliance of the perfect diamond,
His love is the radiance within me,
Brightening my heart and clearing my mind.
I love the instruction of the Lord.

My entire household is full of extraordinary happiness,
Overflowing with the blessings of God.
I am in awe of Him.
I embrace the Lord's code of wisdom.
I make His ways mine.

People who know me rely on my strong moral character.
My children's characters shine with honesty, modesty, and
respectfulness.
A picture of my life would have me bowed on my knees before
the King.
He knights me with the sword of His Spirit and I rise before
Him,
Completely given over to serve His kingdom.

It is easy for those in my family to generate wealth.
We all enjoy a special ability to create and maintain substantial
  riches.
Our businesses, our passions, and even our hobbies are blessed.
Appraisers are always shocked at the high, inherent value of all
  we have.

The legacy of my faith throughout my life will remain.
It will take root in my children, grandchildren, and
  great-grandchildren.
Our family shield declares truthfulness, excellence, and
  prosperity.
We remain firm and unwavering in our purpose, loyalty, and
  resolve to our King.

The light of God's fire burns up the darkness around me,
The light of God's instruction clarifies and purifies my soul,
The light of God's opulence and riches brings me joy—like
  lights on a Christmas tree.

All that I am—
  my inner-being of soul,
  my reason and resolve,
  my conscience and determination,
  my heart and spirit—
Is flooded by His brilliant light.
I shine, refreshed and rested.

——72——
A RIGHT ATTITUDE
(*Psalm 112:5—7*)

I DECREE:

I have made graciousness and consideration of others my
    natural attitude.

My words are straightforward and just,
My actions are fitting and proper for a child of the King.
My heart is full of desire to please the Lord alone,
And because of this my life is level—a straightened path.

Each morning I choose a friendly, generous attitude.
I understand that I don't always know what other people are
    enduring,
So my first reaction is always to offer them the advantage.
I adopt an attitude that honors others and willingly serves their
    needs above my own.

I am careful with my words and actions.
I consider each situation carefully, doing what is proper and
    fitting in each circumstance for business, work, and home.

I have prepared my mind for the day. I set aside selfish
    motivations.
I am confident and content, without a care.
The Lord is my muse and inspiration.
My mind is renewed by His Spirit and presence.

—73—
THE DAY THE LORD MADE
(Psalm 118:24–29)

I DECREE:

I dance around madly, as if no one is watching.
Complete joy and ecstasy are mine.
All because God is with me, He has made this day.
And I know that His purposes will be completed in it.

Before I was born, God fashioned this very day.
He took care and purpose to shape it just for me.
I will conduct myself knowing today is ordained by God.
Today is reason enough to celebrate my life.

Today is the day I enjoy my liberation!
Victory, freedom, deliverance.
Who can fathom God giving aid to man?
I cannot, but I receive it with open arms anyway!

There is no end to the blessings of today.
I am happy, I am prosperous, and my moral character is sure.
God's devotion to me is evident in today's new mercies.
I am overwhelmed by how rich His love is for me.

—74—
LIFE—GOD'S WAY
(Psalm 119:32–40)

I DECREE:

I live my life the way God suggests, and I see it suddenly
   expanding!

My future stretches out before me like the perfect countryside—
It's all pastureland, green fields, and gently flowing rivers.

The journey my life course is set on is the roadway to His
    kingdom.
I know that staying on this path only leads to one place:
Peace with God, peace of mind, and a clear conscience.

I chose this road for a reason, and I am determined to stay on it.
It's an ancient path, a steady and well-traveled way
That has never failed those who walk along its course.

I've come to love this pathway.
I feel life vibrating within me when I stay right in the middle.
It's like being gently shaken on a sifter.
All the harshness of myself separates away,
While all that is pure and fine collects together.

When the path turns, I follow. When it continues straight, so
    do I.
Because of this my heart remains naturally inclined to obey God.
Instinctively, I avoid and shy away from dishonest gain.
I look away from things that only appeal to my vanity and ego.

There is life and breath and freshness in all of God's ways,
And I embrace them with joy and committed passion.
God has set up traffic detours for everything that would
    derail me.
Long before I even get there, shame and disgrace are channeled
    far away.

This journey of life that I walk each day is good.

75

SECURE
(Psalm 125)

I DECREE:

I am confident and secure in You, O Lord.
My confidence is so sure that I am totally fearless before You!
I know my place in You—I am Your highly favored one.
I can ask anything of You, and I come into Your throne room
    every day.

You regard and keep me as Your sacred place, Your Mount
    Zion—
The place where Your chosen bride dwells and waits on You.
I am immovable. In You I cannot shake, slip, or fall.
I am intrepid—unwavering, courageous, and brave.

You are my Jehovah—the one eternally existing, unchanging.
Forever You surround me, encircling me, doubling up round and
    round,
Until the end of the age Your faithfulness to me is sure,
For You are eternal, timeless, and faithful.

Regardless of the actions and behavior of others,
Whether they are ignorant, rebellious, or cruel,
I shall not be compromised in my devotion to the ways of God.
For I hold the scepter of the Lord; I uphold a standard higher
    than theirs.

I am Your delight, Jehovah—I declare it from the mountaintops!
In Your eyes I am beautiful and so much fun to be around.
Like the medicine of laughter, I am the joy in Your day.

I run to You in the spirit, in the cool of the day; I am Yours to
enjoy.

Your thoughts and actions toward me are full of favor.
I am the beneficiary of all that is in You, of all that is good.
You lavish Yourself upon me; You lavish me with the treasures
of heaven.
For in the deepest place of myself, I have chosen to live in
purity.

I decree peace, prosperity, and contentment upon my life.
I decree them upon my children, my home, and my extended
family,
My coworkers, my work, my day, and all who cross my path.
The blessing of the Lord fulfills all my dreams and vision for
life.

———— *76* ————

REST AND PROVISION, EVEN IN SLEEP
(Psalm 127)

I DECREE:

I do not labor in vain; all I work toward is stable and sure.
The house I build is the Lord's.
He planned it and has kept it for me from the beginning.

I follow the Lord's leading, working alongside Him, cooperating
with His Spirit.

I get up early in joy and with gratitude.
I eat the fruit of rest; I feast on peace.
I sleep calmly and peacefully all night long.

The Lord delights in sharing His abundance with me.

He fills my cupboards; He overflows my storehouse.
I am His pride and joy; He withholds nothing from me.

All this, while I sleep the deep, peaceful sleep of one in the arms
of love.

—77—

ALWAYS MORE, ALWAYS HIGHER
(Psalm 128)

I DECREE:

Arise! Arise, thoughts of God's goodness! Arise, words of
adoration!
For the Lord has set aside blessings and immense joy for me:

I am careful with my day and with my time.
I am careful with the presence of the Lord.
I choose words and actions and moods that are inviting to Him.

My life is a journey, and I love the adventure.
I make my way through each day following His lead.
I reap joy in every moment because I smile at every task.

I cannot stop laughing and my days are filled with great friends,
Because I avoid gossip and unkindness and don't cause others
anxiety.
If there is anger, I calm it; if there is sadness, I ease it with care.

My family is my pride and joy, and I love to be with them.
The food in my house multiplies, and my supplies never
diminish.
There is always so much to go around, we cannot stop giving it
away.

Decrees Inspired by the Psalms

My children shine from within—holy, pure, and righteous.
They bring their stories to dinner, and we feast together as
    friends.
They tell me of their dreams and passion, sharing their lives
    with me.

The Lord has blessed me and continues to bless me more every
    day!
My life is filled with beauty, joy, prosperity, property, riches, and
    gladness.

Always more, always higher, always increasing in all that I am,
The peace of lazy, warm summer days is mine every day,
And so it will always be.

—78—

ABUNDANT REDEMPTION
(Psalm 130)

I DECREE:

Adonai, Yahweh, Lord God, Holy One,
You hear me. You listen with careful attention.

Sincere and passionate are Your desires for me.
Joyfully You grant all of my requests.

You follow with proclamations of Your will,
Rendering judgment in my favor.

I wait patiently on Your timing.
Confident. Expectant.

Knowing full well that it is Your business and promise
To satisfy my hope.

I BELIEVE IN YOU.

My soul, my inner, deep, secret self,
Where all my hopes and dreams and desires linger,
Breathes patiently, understanding You are here.

For in You, like nowhere else,
I find tenderness and compassion, liberation, and distinction.

You hold in reserve for me
An abundance of redemption.

——79——
THE BLESSING OF UNITY
(Psalm 133)

I DECREE:

I live in unity
With family, with friends, and with all who cross my path.

What a difference it makes!

It is as if the atmosphere is composed with soft songs—
Songs of peace, notes of happiness, and tones of delight.

And in this calm place,
I find His blessings forever.

—80—
I HEAR YOUR LOVING-KINDNESS
(Psalm 143:7—9)

I DECREE:

Without delay, my voice reaches Your ears.
In an instant You hear me.
Immediately You answer!

Before my spirit has time to falter,
Your brilliant countenance flashes before me,
You show Your face compassionately to me.

You whisper softly to me, speaking only of Your
Tenderness, kindness, faithfulness, mercy, and favor—
Such are Your encouragements to me.

It is this perfect love and high regard You have for me
That causes me to trust You—utterly, completely, and securely.
My spirit, once downcast, is carefree and bold again.

You deliver me. Snatching me away from destruction,
Plundering the very ones who intend harm toward me.
Your heart and breath revive me. You overwhelm me with love.

—81—
YOU WALK MY JOURNEY WITH ME
(Psalm 143:10)

I DECREE:

You teach me how to live, act, think, breathe, feel, and behave.
You teach me diligently, expertly, tenderly, and skillfully—all
by example.

All according to Your ways, Your delight, Your goodwill, and Your favor.

With complete and perfect acceptance, You walk my journey with me.

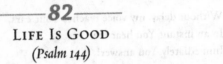

LIFE IS GOOD
(Psalm 144)

I DECREE:

I am blessed of the Lord. I say it again with passion: I am blessed of the Lord!

And I bless the Lord, I bow before Him for He is great and mighty.

My strength, which fuels the momentum of my breakthrough, is from the Lord.

The Lord's sword and arrows are mine, He wields them in my defense.

The Lord's salvation is so beautiful and His protection so sure, I cannot help but sing.

My children are strong and beautiful,
They are promoted in all they put their hands to.
My friends are many and they bear me up.
I am multiplied beyond the borders of my home.

I cannot contain my happiness for all I have in Him!

—— *83* ——
BENEFITS OF THE KINGDOM
(Psalm 144)

I DECREE:

I adore You, Jehovah!
I kneel before You prostrate in Your holy presence,
For You have become my immovable strength.
You are the cleft in the cliff that covers me.

You teach and instruct me in such a way that
When I battle, when I war,
I am accustomed to victory and
In my hand are the spoils and fortunes of war.

You deliver me from those who speak worthless lies,
Whose ways are empty vanities, arrogance, and ego.
Set apart from them, I am separated from toil and lifelessness.
My home, family, business, and spheres of influence are released.

Therefore,

My family is established and distinguished.
My children are caused to be brought up before You,
Able to do great things and to be promoted in all ways,
They are vigorous, passionate, beautiful, and strong!

My business and the works of my hands are promoted
With success and with a good and profitable end.
As full as the seas are with an abundance of water,
So too are my equity, dividends, income, and interest.

Your kingdom produces limitless benefits in me and for me.
I am increased and multiplied exponentially.

My home and business, and the cities where I live are blessed
   with peace.
I abide in You as in a calm retreat.

—— 84 ——

JEHOVAH IS MY GOD!
(Psalm 144:12–15)

I DECREE:

My savings are overflowing! My businesses thrive!
My investments increase in value!

All that I have grows, securing my success,
Enabling me to continue to diversify.

My dividends yield a thousandfold appreciation.
My profits report exponential multiplication.

My friends are faithful and fruitful.
They are strong and have my back.

Wherever I dwell, wherever I travel,
There is no sadness or lack or loss.

Such is the norm for those of us
Who have Jehovah as our God!

— **85** —

BLESS THE LORD
(Psalm 145)

I DECREE:

I bless the Lord. I praise His greatness. I declare His
    faithfulness.

I am grateful beyond measure, and my words are changing the
    atmosphere;

I am creating an open heaven with intent and purpose to live
    there:

Great is the Lord and greatly to be praised.

God is the head of this home.

His ways are my ways.

I put Him on the throne of my heart,

And lift up His faithfulness for everyone to see.

I yield to the Lord.

I bow before Him in holiness.

God's Spirit is within me.

His light shines with incomparable brilliance.

My mind is illuminated from within.

My soul is remade by His clarity and purity

The Lord's size is beyond measure.

His presence—intense beyond bearing

His majesty and beauty cannot be fully known

And yet…

I embrace Him, and He engulfs me.

———— *86* ————
UNLIMITED!
(Psalm 146)

I DECREE:

I unleash my praise to the Lord.
I radiate His Spirit beaming from within me.
I boast in His favor.
I cannot help but sing to Him all day, every day!

I do not rely on the generosity of others.
I do not find security in the world or in men.
They cannot help me.
My hope and provision come from the Lord.
I am so blessed in the riches of God.
He alone is my source.

I can afford to be ridiculously happy because
The One who made heaven and earth is my hope.
His size and greatness and abilities are unlimited.
Therefore my abilities are unlimited because He is in me.
His strength never fails, which means my strength never fails.

These things are true:

God is faithful, and He is faithful to me.
Justice is mine.
I am never hungry; I am always full.
I am never trapped; I am free.

My eyes are open.
I am raised up.
I am loved.
I am protected.

I am supported and provided for.
The wicked around me are thwarted before they even begin.

——87——
HIS GOODNESS INVADES
(Psalm 147)

I DECREE:

My heart is transparent; my soul is clear like glass.
My spirit floats like a feather on the air.
The sound of my voice cuts the atmosphere like a trumpet
As I declare God's goodness.

I enjoy setting aside time to dwell on the beauty and goodness
   of God.
The air is light and fresh. I can taste His presence like misting
   rain.
I am completely preoccupied with Him.

The Lord provides permanent provision, restoring my hope and
   my glory.

My inner man is healed and at peace.
Favor is restored to my home and family.
My businesses thrive because the Lord builds them up.
My extended family and circle of personal friends are
   encouraged.
His goodness invades every moment, every circumstance with
   laughter.

———88———
PRAISE HIM!
(Psalm 148)

I DECREE to creation, to the earth and all its fullness—praise Him!

Praise Him! Praise the Lord God.
For He is the eternal, existing One.

Praise Him from the heavens.
Praise Him from the highest points of earth.
Praise Him from the seats of glory and honor.

All those seated in places of honor and favor and privilege—
    praise Him!

Angels and heavenly hosts, revel in who He is!
Deep space and fountains of the deep, display His wonder!
Sun and sunrise, moon and heavenly bodies, shine with the
    brilliance of His glory!

Boast in His reputation, for He spoke a simple, single command
And all things were fashioned with elegant intricacy.

Boast in His power for He has established His creation forever
And has made a decree that they should never end.

Dragons and beasts dwelling in the abyss and belly of the earth,
    bow before Him!

Elements and seasons, let yourselves go with abandon,
    magnifying His name!

Mountains, hills, valleys, oceans, streams, and waterways, raise
    your voices to His name!

Towering trees, rambling brush, flowering plants, seeds and
  stalks, bloom with His glory!

Every living thing that moves across the earth, roar of His
  majesty!

Nations, leaders, rulers, and judges, command His precepts and
  statutes!

Babes and infants, children and youth, men and women, aged
  and wise,

Act madly making a show of your joy in Him!

Live brilliantly for He alone is above, and He alone is worthy of
  a life invested in Him!

——— **89** ———
HE IS
(Psalm 148:13)

I DECREE:

I boast in the name of the Lord!
I celebrate His renown throughout the ages.

My words and intentions toward Him are clear
His reputation is my stronghold and assurance!

My life, character, and integrity shine brilliantly
Because He is the source of all that I am.

Even if I look foolish to other people, I don't care!
Enjoying the experience of His presence is too much to contain.

Who He is exceeds any thought my mortal mind can conjure.

His realm is inaccessibly high, and yet He dwells within my
heart.

He is and is the source of safety, riches, security, and prosperity.
There is no enemy who can jeopardize His reign.

He is beauty. He is freshness. He is newness.
He is brilliance. He is brightness. He is light. He is, and He is
mine.

Part 2

Decrees Inspired by Selected Hebrew Words From the Psalms

Language is both simple and complex. Words have a face value, but they can have deeper meaning too. They can gain additional meaning from context, cultural idiom, and metaphor. Language is rich, full, and vibrant. And Scripture, as Hebrews 4:12 tells us, "is living and active. Sharper than any double-edged sword, it penetrates even to dividing soul and spirit, joints and marrow; it judges the thoughts and attitudes of the heart" (NIV).

Never has this been more evident than in my study of the Psalms in the original Hebrew language. The ancient Hebrew is both poetic and direct. It is not just prose; it is complex, with full pages comprising mathematical equations.

As I studied the Hebrew for the decrees in this book, I saw that certain words were used over and over, and the expanse of their meaning and the depth of their significance were so striking they deserved a decree all to themselves. Following are decrees inspired by the Hebrew words for "the light," "the way," "to judge," "inheritance," "peace," "increase," "blessed," and "wisdom." They are written so that you can decree the power

> *The ancient Hebrew is both poetic and direct. It is not just prose; it is complex.*

and depth of God's heart and purpose for you over yourself, your life, your family, your business, and your entire sphere of influence.

—— *90* ——
GOD'S LIGHT AND WAY
(Decree inspired by the Hebrew words owr *and*
derek, *as used in Psalm 119:14, 105)*

I DECREE God's light over myself:

The light that shines brightly like the sun
The light that softens the darkness like the moon
The light that brings hope like the dawn
The light that brings warmth like a burning fire.

I decree that the light of God's life is my life.
The light of His instruction is my guide,
The light of His prosperity is my friend, and
The light of His face shines over me.

His light exposes lies and restores truth in my defense.
His light encourages righteousness among all who walk with
    me.
His light brings justice rendered in my favor.

I decree this light shines upon my way:
The journey of life that I travel,
That ancient pathway of God,
The moral character deep within that leads my steps
And my mannerisms, habits and way of being.

—91—
To Judge
*(Decree inspired by the Hebrew word
shaphat, as used in Psalm 7:11)*

I DECREE God as judge over my life.

He is my vindication, my reputation,
The judge of my life.
His government is established over me.

He decides the controversies.
He executes the judgment on my behalf.
He judges and punishes; I do not.

He defends my cause
And enters a judgment in my favor,
Delivering me from all who oppose.

His laws contend on my behalf
And His government brings me peace.
I decree God as judge over my life.

—92—
Inheritance
*(Decree inspired by the Hebrew word
nachalah, as used in Psalm 2:8)*

I DECREE:

I claim the full, redeemed inheritance of my bloodline.
I claim the full and complete inheritance I have in Christ.
I claim it for myself, my family, my children, and my children's
children.
I claim it for generations to come.

The earth is the Lord's and all it contains.
He has transferred the dominion and authority over to me.

All blessings in heavenly places are given to me.
The promised land is mine!

I take possession of the promises of God.
I possess and inhabit the land given to me.
I enjoy all the rights and privileges legally mine.
The heritage of the Lord is at my disposal.

I claim the property as my portion, my cup, and my share.
The harvest is mine.

I am also the inheritance of Christ.
He possesses and inhabits me as His very own.
I am His prized possession, passed down to Him—a gift from
    His Father.

—— 93 ——
PEACE
(Decree inspired by the Hebrew word
shalowm, as used in Psalm 125:5)

I DECREE peace. I make way for peace.

Like a lava tube carved out of rock by the molten lava,
I declare that peace carves out the hard places of my heart and
    makes way for the liquid fire and presence of God.

His peace completes me.
Peace makes my mind sound and my soul to prosper.
Peace creates for me a safe place, a refuge from the world.

My home is a place of tranquility and contentment.
Even though it may be busy, it is a place of rest.
My friends are at ease with me, we enjoy our time together.

My domain and sphere of influence are no longer at war
But prosper in all things, rooted in peace.
I am at peace with God.

——— 94 ———

INCREASE

(Decree inspired by the Hebrew word
yĕbuwl, as used in Psalm 67:6)

I DECREE:

I praise the Lord, and the earth yields its increase. This is a
   promise!

Therefore I praise the Lord.
I praise the Lord in the morning and in the evening.
I praise the Lord when I cannot see His way clearly.
I praise Him when He makes the way known.

Without hesitation and without question
I praise the Lord.

And I am given increase upon increase!
Watch and see how increase overtakes me.

The earth is the Lord's and all it contains.
The earth yields its increase to me by the decree of the Lord!

The whole earth and all it contains—
The land, the soil, and the waterways—yield your increase
   for me.

My home upon the earth, my sphere of influence, my family friends,
Be fruitful, multiply, and yield all your goodness for me.

My business, hobbies, and new opportunities,
I decree increase!

Lost wages—repaid.
Stolen time—restored.
Sales and exchanges—growing.
Work and business—profitable.
Interest and dividend reports—rising.
New ideas and inventions—downloaded.

I speak to the riches of the earth: gold, oil, minerals, and gemstones,
Increase in value, increase in my portfolio, appear in my midst.

I speak to the resources of the earth: water, air, and soil,
Increase in purity and in abundance, increase as my possessions.

I decree the restoration of the earth.
I break the power of the curse and speak freedom!

I speak to the fruit trees and to the seeds planted by the farmer,
Grow, prosper, free of insect and germ, full of life and life-giving power.

I decree nourishment to the earth and welcome nourishment in return.

I praise the Lord, for all that He does for me.
I praise the Lord for the increase granted to me.

——95——

BLESSED

(Decree Inspired by the Hebrew word
barak, *as used in Psalm 67:7)*

I DECREE the blessing of the Lord!

I decree that God has blessed me, and His blessings are such that the entire ends of the earth quake and are in fear because of His goodness to me.

The favor that shines upon me as a child of Jehovah is unlike anything bestowed by an earthly father.

I bend my knee in order to receive the ordination and blessing of my Lord. He causes me to kneel, encouraging and enabling me to lie prostrate before Him in peace.

Dripping from His words are peace and safety. He is my crown and shield.

His blessing moves in and through and beyond me, catching me up in a wake of His favor. He speaks to me in the night seasons, bringing His clear counsel and instruction.

His words are eternally and divinely inspired, carrying with them the gifts of heaven.

His blessing vibrates within my very being, a living vibrant echo of His countenance, bringing me into a true knowledge of who He is and into a present experience of true worship.

96

WISE WISDOM

(Decree inspired by the Hebrew words chokmah, sekel/
sakal, *as used in Psalms 2:10; 14:2; 32:8; 53:2; 111:10)*

I DECREE the wisdom and understanding of the Spirit of God.

The all-knowing spirit of wisdom
Imparts to me the ability to understand perfectly!

Prudent in action and circumspect of heart,
Such is the wise wisdom of the Lord:

Full of sense and discretion,
Bringing insight and deepening meaning.

Wise wisdom causes prosperity,
And with knowledge of Him comes success.

Part 3

Decrees Inspired by Psalm 24 to Influence Culture for the Kingdom of Heaven

THERE ARE SEATS of power that influence human culture. They extend beyond the boundaries of what is considered Western or Eastern culture or the status of a first-world or third-world nation. These "influencers" shape the way a people view the world and their place in it.

These seats of power are less about world governments, systems, and programs and more about the spiritual forces operating in the invisible realm. As Ephesians 6:12 explains, "We are not fighting against flesh-and-blood enemies, but against evil rulers and authorities of the unseen world, against mighty powers in this dark world, and against evil spirits in *heavenly places*" (NLT, emphasis added).

In the Word we often see seats of power referred to as "hills," "mountains," and "high places." These seats can belong to dark forces, as described in Deuteronomy 12:2, "Destroy all the places where they worship their gods—high on the mountains, up on the hills" (NLT). Or they can depict places the Lord inhabits, as in Psalm 15:1, "Who may worship in your sanctuary, LORD? Who may enter your presence on your *holy hill?*" (NLT, emphasis added). Whether these seats of power, or high places, are occupied and controlled by the kingdom of darkness or the kingdom of heaven determines the kind of cultural influence they have.

In order to combat the dark forces that are operating and

influencing the world and the people in it, we employ spiritual tools. One of those tools is decrees. Through this simple yet powerfully effective spiritual tool we can change our lives, families, work, and spheres of influence and cause the kingdom of heaven to reign in and over every seat of power.

Psalm 24:1 tells us "The earth is the LORD's, and everything in it, the world and all its people belong to him" (NLT). Since the world and all it contains belong to the Lord, we have authority over it. Therefore, when we decree His Word, we are able to release His kingdom as the dominating cultural influence. We establish His kingdom—God's realm—in the seats of power.

> *Through this simple yet powerfully effective spiritual tool we can cause the kingdom of heaven to reign in and over every seat of power.*

The chief influencers in our culture have been identified as follows: business, government, family, religion, media, education, and entertainment. These are the seats of power that have the greatest impact upon cultural mind-sets—the way people think—and upon cultural trends.

In the following pages Psalm 24 has been adapted as a decree addressing each of these seats of power. Psalm 24:3 identifies God's place as a "mountain," and these decrees continue that metaphor with the intent to establish God as *the* cultural influencer. Micah 4:1 prophesies that this will happen:

> In the last days it shall come to pass, that the mountain of the house of the LORD shall be established in the top of the mountains, and it shall be exalted above the hills; and people shall flow unto it.

Together we can decree over the seats of power in the heavenly places and see each of the seven cultural influencers won back for God!

——97——
A DECREE FOR BUSINESS

I DECREE:

This mountain is the Lord's!

Business and all of its purposes were designed and established by God.

All those who dwell upon this marketplace mountain are the Lord's.

We claim them for His righteousness.

We acknowledge the olive tree planted by the Lord atop this mountain.

We declare the anointing of the Lord dwells upon the business seat of power.

We release His anointing, His purposes, His Spirit, His business, His increase,

His prosperity, His blessing, favor, and grace.

We who love the Lord, who love "being about the Father's business,"

We resolve to ascend this business mountain!

Our faith is pure. Our mind is set on Christ.

With our hands we wield the power and victory of the Most High.

We declare that we cannot be bought or sold.

Our inner, secret self is sincere in the pursuit of honesty, integrity, and righteousness.

Our conscience and emotions are without compromise,
    reflecting His pure light.
We are strong and full of courage.

We have the blessing of the Lord. His devotion is set toward us.
He has lavished us with gifts upon gifts upon gifts.
We release them upon this mountain.

The Lord has a peace treaty for the business mountain.
His desire is to restore the mountain to its original intent and
    purpose.
We establish it for Him.

The time has come. We are the generation, the people who seek
    His face.
We are the dwelling place of the Most High.
We wrestle with the promise, and we wrestle for the promise.
We set our hands and will not let go until this seat of power is
    ours!

Hey! You portals of business, inventions, strategies, and
    blueprints;
You gates of entryway; you marketplace and public meeting
    places;
You ancient doors and passageways of hope; you mouthpieces of
    the heavens,
We decree over you!

Be awakened! Lift up your heads, open up, and be released.
Receive a new blueprint and agenda.
Receive the heart of the Father and His business.
Be restored to the foundation of your Creator and your purpose!

Make yourselves ready.

The King of glory, splendor, dignity, honor, and riches is ready to pass through.

The Lord of the angel armies, of all creation, the God of war is upon you.

— 98 —

A DECREE FOR GOVERNMENT

I DECREE:

This mountain is the Lord's!

All governmental seats of power, all ruling high places

Your foundations and purposes were designed and established by God

All those who dwell upon the government mountain are the Lord's.

We claim them for His righteousness.

We acknowledge the olive tree planted by the Lord atop this mountain.

We declare the anointing of the Lord dwells upon all governmental seats of power

We release His anointing, His purposes, His Spirit, and His government.

We who love the Lord, who love His government, order, and authority

Resolve to ascend this government mountain!

Our faith is pure. Our mind is set on Christ.

With our hands we wield the power and victory of the Most High.

We declare that we cannot be bought or sold. We are not
 vulnerable to lobbying.
Our inner, secret self is sincere in the pursuit of right
 government, right rule.
Our conscience and emotions are without compromise,
 reflecting His pure light.
We are strong and full of courage.

We have the blessing of the Lord. His devotion is set toward us.
He has lavished us with gifts upon gifts upon gifts.
We release them upon this mountain.

The Lord has a peace treaty for the government mountain.
His desire is to restore the mountain to its original intent and
 purpose.
We establish it for Him.

The time has come. We are the generation, the people who seek
 His face.
We are the dwelling place of the Most High.
We wrestle with the promise, and we wrestle for the promise.
We set our hands and will not let go until this government
 mountain is ours!

Hey! You portals of authority, leadership, rule, and government;
You gates of entryway, law forums, and public meeting places;
You ancient doors and passageways of hope; you mouthpieces of
 the heavens,
We decree over you!

Be awakened. Lift up your heads, open up, and be released.
Receive a new blueprint and agenda.
Receive Spirit-led leadership.
Be restored to the foundation of your Creator and your purpose!

Make yourselves ready.

The King of glory, splendor, dignity, honor, and riches is ready to pass through.

The Lord of the angel armies, of all creation, the God of war is upon you.

——— 99 ———

A DECREE FOR FAMILY

I DECREE:

This mountain is the Lord's!

Family, as a place of safety and unity, as a model of love and strength,

All of its purposes were designed and established by God.

All those who dwell upon this family mountain are the Lord's.

We claim them for His righteousness.

We acknowledge the olive tree planted by the Lord atop this mountain.

We speak life, liberty, fruitfulness, and eternity to this tree.

We declare the anointing of the Lord dwells upon all familial seats of power.

We release His anointing, His purposes, and His Spirit.

We release His love, His unity, and His brotherhood and sisterhood.

We who love the Lord, who love being a part of the family of God,

We resolve to ascend this family mountain!

Our faith is pure. Our mind is set on Christ. We are one.

With our hands we wield the power and victory of the Most High.

We declare that we are for Christ, His family, and His body.
  We are for unity.
Our inner, secret self is sincere in the pursuit of faith, hope, and
  love.
Our conscience and emotions are steady, without competition or
  jealousy,
Reflecting His pure light. We are strong and full of courage.

We decree over this mountain the fruit of the Spirit:
Love, joy, peace, patience, kindness, goodness, faithfulness,
  gentleness, and self-control.
We decree the nature of love over the family mountain and over
  our families.
We decree patience and kindness and cut off envy, boasting, and
  striving.
We decree humility and cut off rudeness and self-centered
  attitudes.
We make room only for righteous anger, but keep no record of
  wrongs.
The family mountain rejoices in truth.
We decree an atmosphere where love always protects, trusts,
  hopes, and believes the best. Love perseveres.
The family mountain is rich in the love that will never fail.

We have the blessing of the Lord. His devotion is set toward us.
He has lavished us with gifts upon gifts upon gifts.
We release them upon this mountain.

The Lord has a peace treaty for the family mountain.
His desire is to restore the mountain to its original intent and
  purpose.
We establish it for Him.

The time has come. We are the generation, the people who seek
His face.

We are the dwelling place of the Most High.

We wrestle with the promise, and we wrestle for the promise.

We set our hands and will not let go until this family mountain
is ours!

Hey! You portals of protection; you gateways of love, unity, and
intimacy;

You covering places; you ancient doors and passageways of hope;

You mouthpieces of the heavens,

We decree over you!

Be awakened. Lift up your heads, open up, and be released.

Receive a new blueprint and agenda.

Be the thoroughfare of His peace.

Be restored to the foundation of your Creator and your purpose!

Make yourselves ready.

The King of glory, splendor, dignity, honor, and riches is ready
to pass through.

The Lord of the angel armies, of all creation, the God of war is
upon you.

—100—

A DECREE FOR RELIGION

I DECREE:

This mountain is the Lord's!

Religion in purest form of worship and service,

All of its purposes were designed and established by God.

All those who dwell upon this sacred mountain are the Lord's.

We claim them for His righteousness.

We acknowledge the olive tree planted by the Lord atop this mountain

We speak truth, purity, honesty, wise counsel, and accuracy to the tree.

We declare the anointing of the Lord dwells upon all religious seats of power

We release His anointing, His purposes, and His Spirit. We release truth.

We decree the sevenfold Spirit of God over all religious high places:

The Spirit of the Fear of the Lord

The Spirit of Wisdom and Knowledge

The Spirit of Revelation and Prophecy

The Spirit of Counsel and the Spirit of Truth

The Spirit of Might and Power

We decree the reign of the Holy Spirit!

We who love the Lord also love the widows and orphans, for this is true religion.

We resolve to ascend this religion mountain for them!

Our faith is pure. Our mind is set on Christ.

With our hands we wield the power and victory of the Most High.

We declare that we will not be deceived.

Our inner, secret self is sincere in the pursuit of love, hope, and charity.

Our conscience and emotions are without compromise, reflecting His pure light.

We are strong and full of courage.

We have the blessing of the Lord. His devotion is set toward us.
He has lavished us with gifts upon gifts upon gifts.
We release them upon this mountain.

The Lord has a peace treaty for the religion mountain.
His desire is to restore the mountain to its original intent and
purpose.
We establish it for Him.

The time has come. We are the generation, the people who seek
His face.
We are the dwelling place of the Most High.
We wrestle with the promise, and we wrestle for the promise.
We set our hands and will not let go until all religious high
places are ours!

Hey! You spirit portals; you gates of entryway; you sacred and
holy places;
You ancient doors and passageways of truth and faith;
You mouthpieces of the heavens, we decree over you!

Be awakened. Lift up your heads, open up, and be released.
Receive a new blueprint and agenda; receive truth and love.
Be restored to the foundation of your Creator and your purpose!

Make yourselves ready.
The King of glory, splendor, dignity, honor, and riches is ready
to pass through.
The Lord of the angel armies, of all creation, the God of war is
upon you.

—101—
A Decree for Media

I decree:

This mountain is the Lord's!

Media in all its forms and all of its purposes were designed and established by God.

All those who dwell upon this media mountain are the Lord's.

We claim them for His righteousness.

We acknowledge the olive tree planted by the Lord atop this mountain.

We declare the anointing of the Lord dwells upon the media mountain.

We release His anointing, His purposes, His Spirit, and His media.

We who love the Lord and His media resolve to ascend this mountain!

Our faith is pure. With our hands we wield the power and victory of the Most High.

Our mind is set on Christ. Our inner, secret self is sincere in the pursuit of truth.

Our conscience and emotions are without compromise, reflecting His pure light.

We are strong and full of courage.

We have the blessing of the Lord. His devotion is set toward us.

He has lavished us with gifts upon gifts upon gifts.

We release them upon this mountain.

The Lord has a peace treaty for the media mountain.

His desire is to restore the mountain to its original intent and
purpose.

We establish it for Him.

The time has come. We are the generation, the people, who seek
His face.

We are the dwelling place of the Most High.

We wrestle with the promise, and we wrestle for the promise.

We set our hands and will not let go until this media mountain
is ours!

Hey! You portals of media and gates of entryway, you
information highways,

Whether Internet, satellite, gaming, social, educational, or
news,

You ancient doors and passageways of hope; you mouthpieces of
the heavens,

We decree over you!

Be awakened! Lift up your heads, open up, and be released.

Receive a new blueprint and agenda.

Be restored to the foundation of your Creator and your purpose!

Make yourselves ready.

The King of glory, splendor, dignity, honor, and riches is ready
to pass through.

The Lord of the angel armies, of all creation, the God of war is
upon you.

——102——
A DECREE FOR EDUCATION

I DECREE:

This mountain is the Lord's!

Education and all of its purposes were designed and established
by God

All those who dwell upon this education mountain are the
Lord's.

We claim them for His righteousness.

We acknowledge the olive tree planted by the Lord atop this
mountain.

We declare the anointing and peace of the Lord dwells upon the
education high places.

We release His anointing, His purposes, His Spirit, and His
education.

We speak the wisdom of the Lord and the knowledge of the
holy One.

We who love the Lord and His discipleship resolve to ascend
this mountain!

Our faith is pure. Our mind is set on Christ.

Our inner, secret self is sincere in the pursuit of truth.

With our hands we wield the power and victory of the Most
High.

Our conscience and emotions are without compromise,
reflecting His pure light.

We are strong and full of courage.

We have the blessing of the Lord. His devotion is set toward us.

He has lavished us with gifts upon gifts upon gifts.

We release them upon this mountain.

The Lord has a peace treaty for the education mountain.

His desire is to restore the mountain to its original intent and purpose.

We establish it for Him.

The time has come. We are the generation, the people who seek His face.

We are the dwelling place of the Most High.

We wrestle with the promise, and we wrestle for the promise.

We set our hands and will not let go until this education mountain is ours!

Hey! You portals of truth and learning; you gates of entryway;

You places of education and mentoring; you portals of the agora and high places;

You ancient doors and passageways of hope; you mouthpieces of the heavens,

We decree over you!

Be awakened, lift up your heads, open up, and be released.

Be released from deception and lies, and be purified.

Be released of false agendas, and receive a new blueprint and agenda.

We decree that only truth can flow through you.

We cut off deception, lies, and wisdom of the world.

We cut off questioning against God's authority and truth.

We decree the fear of the Lord,

His wisdom and understanding, and His revelation and prophecy.

We decree over education, be restored to the foundation of your Creator and your purpose!

Make yourselves ready.

The King of glory, splendor, dignity, honor, and riches is ready
to pass through.

The Lord of the angel armies, of all creation, the God of war is
upon you.

—103—

A DECREE FOR ENTERTAINMENT

I DECREE:

This mountain is the Lord's!

Entertainment and all of its purposes were designed and
established by God.

All those who dwell upon this entertainment mountain are the
Lord's.

We claim them for His righteousness.

We acknowledge the olive tree planted by the Lord atop this
mountain

We declare the anointing, peace, and unity of the Lord dwell
upon the entertainment high places.

We release His anointing, His purposes, and His Spirit.

We decree His laughter, His joy, fun, and delight. We release
His entertainment.

We who love the Lord and His presence resolve to ascend this
mountain!

Our faith is pure. Our mind is set on Christ.

Our inner, secret self is sincere in the pursuit of purity.

With our hands we wield the power and victory of the Most
High.

Our conscience and emotions are without compromise,
  reflecting His delight.
We are strong and full of courage.

We have the blessing of the Lord. His devotion is set toward us.
He has lavished us with gifts upon gifts upon gifts.
We release them upon this mountain.

The Lord has a peace treaty for the entertainment mountain.
His desire is to restore the mountain to its original intent and
  purpose.
We establish it for Him.

We speak purity and purification over the entertainment
  mountain.
We wash you with the Word of the Lord; we bless you in His
  name.
We decree the restoration of the joy of the Lord and the
  pleasure and rest of God.

The time has come. We are the generation, the people who seek
  His face.
We are the dwelling place of the Most High.
We wrestle with the promise, and we wrestle for the promise.
We set our hands and will not let go until this entertainment
  mountain is ours!

Hey! You portals of entertainment; you gates of entryway;
You marketplace and public meeting places;
You ancient doors and passageways of hope; and you
  mouthpieces of the heavens,
We decree over you!

Be awakened. Lift up your heads, open up, and be released.
Receive a new blueprint and agenda.

We shut down portals of perversion.

We destroy wickedness, vulgarity, and mammon.

We destroy the spirits that lure God's children into dark places and secrecy.

We speak life and revelation over the portals of entertainment!

Receive joy, fun, and laughter from the throne room.

Be purified, invigorated, and inspired.

Be restored to the foundation of your Creator and your purpose!

Make yourselves ready.

The King of glory, splendor, dignity, honor, and riches is ready to pass through.

The Lord of the angel armies, of all creation, the God of war is upon you.

From Elizabeth A. Nixon, Esq., author of
Inspired by the Psalms, Decrees That Renew Your Heart and Mind:

Ephesians 2:10 tells us that, "We are His workmanship, created in Christ Jesus for good works, which God prepared beforehand so that we should walk in them" (NASB). Hebrews 12 encourages us to "run the race", or as it may also be translated, "live the life appointed and destined for us". These verses speak to us about our highest spiritual calling, that is our destiny, which is to walk in the purpose that God specifically made for us, and made us for. When we live this life, we live life full of passion, joy, peace, health, abundance, fulfillment, satisfaction and success -- both in the natural and the supernatural realms. We walk in the fulfillment of The Lord's Prayer, "Thy Kingdom come, Thy Will be done, in earth as it is in Heaven" (KJV).

Not only does the Bible tell us about the availability of this kind of life, it also contains details about the specific ways that God designed to help us step into it. Elizabeth A. Nixon, Esq., and White Quill Media have created DVD and CD resources that take these spiritual tools and put them in easy-to-understand terms so that you can incorporate them into your every day life. These resources and materials are designed to enable and empower you to step into your highest spiritual calling. You will be launched into your destiny!

Titles available to help launch you into your destiny include *The Destiny Series*:
- *The Power of Decrees*
- *Living in the Rhythm of Heaven*
- *The Desires of Your Heart*

Find these and more at www.WhiteQuillMedia.com.
"Like" on Facebook at www.Facebook.com/WhiteQuillMedia.
Follow on Twitter at www.twitter.com/WhiteQuillMedia.

Elizabeth is married to Jonathan Nixon, author of *Angel Stories*.
They have been married for 28 years and have a 5-year-old son, Joshua.
Together they all enjoy sailing catamarans and off-road Jeep adventures.

WHITE QUILL
M E D I A